PRAISE FOR

ONE KENSINGTON

'Speaks to a lost London barely recognisable in the more staid, corporate landscape today'

Sunday Times

'A brutal exposé . . . written with furious personal compassion for those let down. It is a deconstruction of the culture that ultimately led to some of the failures at Grenfell Tower and is absolutely damning from start to finish'

Peter Apps, *Inside Housing*

'An eye-opening, breath-taking and damning indictment of the divisions that rend this country . . . required reading for anyone who wishes to understand the pressing case for meaningful local democracy – and how far Britain falls short of it'

Morning Star

Emma Dent Coad was born in London to an Anglo-Spanish family. She spent 30 years as a journalist writing about design and architecture, specialising in social housing and planning. She is a life-long political activist, and has been involved in numerous campaigns over the years related to social issues. She joined Kensington and Chelsea Council as a Labour Councillor in 2006. Her surprise election as the first Labour MP for Kensington on 9 June 2017, by 20 votes, overturned a majority of 7,331 and made her a national figure. Four days later the atrocity of the fire at Grenfell Tower, near her home, set the tone for her time in Westminster. During her time in Westminster Emma was an outspoken advocate for her Kensington constituents, particularly on numerous issues related to Grenfell. She remains a campaigner and Labour Councillor in Kensington and Chelsea.

ONE KENSINGTON

FOOD HALLS, FOOD BANKS AND GRENFELL:
INSIDE THE MOST UNEQUAL BOROUGH IN BRITAIN

Emma Dent Coad

QUERCUS

First published in Great Britain in 2022 by Quercus Editions Ltd
This paperback published in 2023 by

QUERCUS

Quercus Editions Ltd
Carmelite House
50 Victoria Embankment
London EC4Y 0DZ

An Hachette UK company

A CIP catalogue record for this book is available
from the British Library

PB ISBN 978 1 52941 725 8
Ebook ISBN 978 1 52941 726 5

10 9 8 7 6 5 4 3 2 1

Typeset by CC Book Production
Printed and bound in Great Britain by Clays Ltd, Elcograf S.p.A.

MIX
Paper | Supporting
responsible forestry
FSC www.fsc.org **FSC® C104740**

Papers used by Quercus are from well-managed forests and other responsible sources.

I dedicate this book to the bereaved and survivors of the Grenfell Tower fire, and all their neighbours and friends who continue to be severely affected by this atrocity on our doorstep. Also, to the hundreds of thousands of tenants and leaseholders around the country living in buildings that are not fire-safe, living in fear every day that there could be a Grenfell 2. Alongside the fight for safe and healthy homes is the fight for justice for the seventy-two, which still seems beyond reach after five painful years.

CONTENTS

PREFACE

This book is not a polite discourse on the indefensible extremes of inequality that prevail in the Royal Borough of Kensington and Chelsea (RBKC), 'the most unequal borough in Britain'. Instead, it aims to provide a painstakingly evidenced case, gathered in person over many years, that reveals the actions and motivations of the Council responsible for the ongoing existence of inequity, which some believe has been deliberately fostered to drive low-income families out of the borough. The Council is backed by huge financial reserves and had a breathtaking programme for the redevelopment of Council estates. This ill-conceived plan, followed over many years, preceded the worst peacetime disaster of our time, the Grenfell Tower fire.

On the morning of 14 June 2017, seventy-two of my neighbours burned to death in their homes, in front of their community, family and friends, who watched helplessly for eighteen hours while overstretched emergency services worked beyond exhaustion to save lives and douse the fire. After the fire, while Kensington's disparate communities and near neighbours came forward to give their help freely and tirelessly, the Council was nowhere to be seen.

The Council that had ignored warnings that this fire could happen.

The Council that had sent 'cease and desist' letters to those warning them.

The Council now facing corporate manslaughter charges.

This book is written from my personal perspective. This comes from my experience of living in the borough, my sixteen years serving on the Council in numerous roles on most of the committees, serving on the Labour Group as Secretary, Chair and Leader, and my observations of the Council's decision-making – financial and ideological – that preceded the fire, and of the chaos afterwards, which turned a tragedy into an atrocity. It is written with unremitting anger and frustration.

Was this disaster due to the Council's incompetence? To disdain for social tenants? To warped spending priorities? To years of deregulation and underspending on social housing? Or was it just bad luck?

I hope this book will give you the information you need to decide for yourself. It has been written partly to vent my anger, and partly to give an insider's view of the bizarre mechanics of the RBKC Council. Of course, I have my own views on the accountability of the Council; nonetheless, here I have tried my utmost to present factual information dispassionately.

This book also looks at the communities that make Kensington and Chelsea so very special. In it I talk of my ambition to encourage these communities to lead the way out of the continuing chaos. These communities should rightly gain recognition as equal partners, as the true leaders, in the ongoing post-Grenfell recovery.

The Council's motto is *Quam bonum in unum habitare*: 'how good it is to dwell in unity' (from Psalm 133). That is also my wish. But a Council that offers 'all cherry, no cake', a Council addicted to vanity projects while ignoring multiple deprivation, even food poverty, has a long way to go.

The Council's 'Efficiency Plan 2016–17' stated its mission:

> We want the Royal Borough to be a place where people of all backgrounds wish to live: an attractive, safe and diverse area in which residents, businesses and visitors have the opportunity to thrive; a place that is smart, creative and prosperous, with resilient and public-spirited residents who respect their neighbours and contribute to their local communities.

Instead Kensington and Chelsea will always be known as the borough where 'efficiency savings' led to the loss of seventy-two lives, and cost the public purse £1 billion.

Many years ago I was living in social housing, in a property that suffered from damp and mould. I warned my landlord many times that this damp and mould made my home unsafe. I was ignored. Then my ceiling collapsed, narrowly missing my daughter's head. This was the start of a five-year legal battle. At the time, a friend told me that if I made contemporaneous notes of meetings, and dated and signed these, that they could be submitted as evidence in a court of law. This advice led me to begin a habit of making notes: this habit has served me well over the years. I keep them all.

All statistics, times, quotes and analyses in this book are given in good faith and made with the benefit gained from sixteen years of careful note-taking and observation during hundreds – if not thousands – of committee and Council meetings. All the Council documents I have quoted from are in the public domain; I have not used my access to Part B confidential papers, or to Part B confidential meetings which are shared privately with Councillors. Nothing here breaks confidentiality.

This book was written in late 2021, during the final stages of the Grenfell Tower Inquiry. It was published soon after the Inquiry's conclusion but before its final report was released: it reflects my perspective of the situation at the time. This timing is deliberate, to avoid any accusations of interference. The facts in this book have been checked, and any errors are just that. I have no need to invent, exaggerate or misinterpret. The truth speaks for itself, and is shocking enough.

Any profits from this book will be distributed to the local charities that have been so badly served by the Council. Anything less would dishonour the dead of Grenfell. I dedicate this book to the survivors, the bereaved, and everyone affected by the atrocity of the Grenfell Tower fire, which happened on our doorstep, and to the hundreds of thousands of people across the country who fear that Grenfell II could happen to them.

INTRODUCTION

I was spanked by a nun on my first day of school. I was spanked on the main landing in front of the whole school as pupils were going downstairs at breaktime.

My unspeakable crime? I missed my mother, and was crying.

The humiliation and pain of that day stayed with me for years. I became shy and withdrawn. Recently I found and framed one of my school reports, written when I was ten, and put it by my front door. The headmistress wrote: 'Margaret Mary [my baptismal name] is very steady and has an unusual sense of responsibility. She is a bright, intelligent pupil, yet becomingly unobtrusive.'

Becomingly unobtrusive? I have done my best over the years to overturn that damning verdict.

I was born in Chelsea in 1954, in Paultons Square off King's Road, which was a proper family neighbourhood and very mixed. My father's job as a hospital doctor supported my mother, six children and my Spanish granny. An NHS doctor couldn't possibly afford to live in Chelsea supporting nine people today.

I remember well the Bluebird Garage, the old tramlines where a tiny foot could get caught, neighbours walking down the street in their dressing gowns to catch the early post. There was a lavender seller, a French onion-seller on a bicycle festooned with onions, babies left in their prams by their doorsteps for their afternoon snooze 'to give them an airing', front doors open much of the day for children to run in and out, chalked hopscotch patterns on the pavement, and men with ladders and long tapers lighting gaslights. There was Boris the grocers, where we children were given little paper bags so we could raid the broken biscuit jar.

Today, these are all gone.

Today I can see why Chelsea was so popular with families and why it was such a good place to grow up for me: it was down to good neighbourhood planning. Good planning should be invisible, but should make daily life convenient, comfortable and safe. A well-planned neighbourhood will have everything you need within a ten-minute walk: a post office, GP surgery, dentist, pharmacy, transport links, schools and nurseries, hairdresser and dry cleaner. You might want the kind of corner shop where you could run a tab for a few days or have a friendly chat, where the shopkeepers know that, for some people, that could be their only human interaction all day. Many good shopkeepers will keep an eye on older or frail customers, and offer to deliver some basics if the pavements are icy and treacherous, or if you are ill, or you have a poorly child. All these things make neighbourhoods work and serve the people who live there. That's why we fight to protect them.

Where I live now, in North Kensington, is precisely like old Chelsea. If you can't start your car, a neighbour will run out with jump leads or send their son out to give you a push. You can call the corner shop if you're ill, and they will bring supplies. Ours gives us some bubbly at Christmas; we bring them a hot Christmas lunch. 'The gravy was good this year' – the cheek of it! There are numerous tight-knit neighbourhoods around the borough, but over the years many have been eroded or are in danger.

Kensington and Chelsea is now a magnet for those who are happy to gut our neighbourhoods to replace them with depositories for international money. Of course we welcome improvements – such as step-free access at Knightsbridge Tube station – but let's see just how many of the offices, shops and homes that are currently being built are occupied after years of relentless nuisance caused by construction works. Where is the benefit to local people? All too often we are subjected to the cuckoo effect, whereby people drop their money into our neighbourhoods and leave, while we unwittingly nurture it, displacing our own chicks as house prices soar.

As the spanking incident showed, discipline at my primary school was strict. For me, the greatest legacy of this school was meeting my international classmates. A small private Catholic school in South Kensington, it attracted the children of diplomats and even foreign royalty. I had friends from all corners of the world. I thought they were all beautiful, with gorgeous hair, so different to mine. My Polish friends had looped plaits reaching to their waists; a Japanese friend had a thick, glossy ink-black single plait; the South American girls had long brown plaits or ponytails; and one Yoruba princess had a stunning fluffy Afro. In comparison, I was tall and gawky for my age with a sensible bob. I felt very English and boring. As a consequence of my early experience at school, plus the parade of international colleagues my father invited home who became instant aunties and uncles, I had no concept whatever of the supposed

3

ethnic hierarchy until it was explained to me in my teens. I still don't get it – on whose planet are we all not considered equal? But I also acknowledge that it is a privilege for me not to 'get it'. Racism always shocks me, and I fight discrimination – wherever it comes from.

Virgo Fidelis may have done little for my self-esteem, but the education it gave me was good. Afterwards, rather than follow my four sisters to Sacred Heart Hammersmith, I spent three unedifying years at a small Catholic secondary school in Ealing, where we had moved from Chelsea to get a larger house and garden. The nuns there did not win my respect. It was poor educationally and I was way ahead of my classmates. I quickly got bored. Then naughty. I became disruptive. I played pranks. The classrooms were interconnected, and one day I removed some screws from the doors so they hung crooked and wouldn't close. Total chaos – we could hear teachers yelling at their classes from one end of the school to the other. They never found out who did it. When we misbehaved, one teacher had a habit of crossing her arms and sucking in her cheeks while fixing us with a steely glare. It was hilarious. A group of us used to provoke her deliberately so she'd make the face. One day I just couldn't stop laughing so she sent me out of the room. I was so helpless with laughter I had to crawl, tears pouring down my face.

It was time for a change. My mother eventually moved me to Sacred Heart but the rot had set in. I made good friends there, some lifelong, but I had lost my earlier focus. Instead, I continued my prankster career. Some of us took particularly against student teachers and would provoke them until they cried. We were horrible. One day we put a battery radio under some loose floorboards

4

in the classroom. The teacher came in and said, 'Turn off the radio'. We all said 'What radio?' She got very cross and searched the entire classroom, while we pretended not to hear anything. Then she left the room to fetch the headmistress. We, of course, turned off the radio and sat there, all innocence, and the headmistress was most annoyed with the teacher.

Our music teacher, Mr Buckley, was very irritating. I used to play up in his classes quite a lot. One day he sent me out of the music room for some misdemeanour. As I left I saw that the key was in the door, on the outside, so I locked them in. It took a while for him to persuade one of the girls to climb out of the window and run round to unlock the door. I was punished for this by having to polish the quad with a huge floor-polisher. It took two hours but it was worth it: I was a hero.

Our English teacher, Mrs Colsell, was another one who annoyed me a lot. She had taught my four older sisters, and constantly reminded me of how good they had been compared to me. She was a large woman, heavily corseted. One day I went a bit too far. I put several thumb tacks, points up, on her chair. I imagined that she would sit down, then scream, jump up and run out of the room. But no. She felt nothing. At the end she left the room, thumb tacks clearly visible in her backside. That was some corset.

The one saving grace for me was Mother Bunbury. She was remarkable for a Catholic nun in the 1970s, and as headmistress she changed the whole atmosphere of the school. For some reason, we clicked. She was liberal, intelligent, funny and engaging. If we were caught running in the corridors, we had to write a limerick about it – and it had to make her laugh or we'd have to rewrite it. She was frankly odd-looking, but her beatific smile and sense of humour made her very attractive. She had two budgerigars, Ham and Smith, and she used to whistle to them. It was very impressive.

Mother Bun – as we called her – told us something I will never forget: 'Read everything, go to everything, and make up your own mind.'

I have never forgotten this, and I practise this to this day.

When I was in fifth form, a group of us joined the National Union of School Students (NUSS, a brief interlude in NUS history) and went on strike. We wanted to ban school uniform and homework, and get pocket money in sixth form. We skipped classes and sat in the quad. The nuns went off for tea, and sent out for buns. Clearly a serious discussion was taking place. Some time later, Mother Bunbury appeared. She suggested we set up a Sixth Form Council where we could debate these matters. We did so. This led to the abolition of school uniform for sixth formers, but the agreement that we should all wear blue to school – quite a victory for 1972. We also set up a debating society. Mother Bunbury encouraged us to get involved in the broiling political melee of the early 1970s. One day a group of us trooped off to a meeting in Portobello Road. It seemed to be run by Maoists, who were handing out Chinese propaganda. Door security had been supplied by local members of the Black Panthers movement. They spotted an infiltrator and threw him out – Richard Neville of *Oz* magazine. It was an exhilarating time.

After this, my political education continued: I joined the National Union of Students at college and uni, the National Union of Journalists when I began writing for magazines, then Unite when I became a Councillor. I have continued to be involved with fighting for justice and equality in education: I was delighted to be invited by my old uni, the Royal College of Art, to speak at a University College Union strike picket, and have spoken at Imperial College to support striking staff. Every campaign needs a range of voices, and I've spoken numerous times for causes including CND (Campaign for Nuclear Disarmament), Stop the War, Stand Up to Racism, and Republic. To me, all these issues are important – and connected.

So why have I focused my fury – in this book – on RBKC Council? My fury has built up over a lifetime. The Council has wasted our money. It was deliberate. The Council cut corners on the Grenfell Tower refurbishment. The Council knew what they were doing, and their actions led to the most horrific and avoidable loss of life. I want you to see what happened through my eyes.

For me, since this is where I grew up, it's personal.

To introduce what some people have suggested is the rank financial incompetence of RBKC Council, I'll explain the first time I became aware of it. After living in Ealing for a period, then – after getting divorced – in a squat in Islington for two years, then a 'hard to let' high-rise in Bermondsey, I had returned to the beautiful borough to have a family. It must have been around 1988 – because my first-born was in a buggy – when I first ventured out to Portobello Market. In an attempt to boost trade by giving the street an olde-worlde feel, the Council had decided to lay cobblestones along the entire length of the market. This genius idea came from the then Cabinet Member for the Environment, who was Leader of the Council at the time of the Grenfell Tower fire.

No discussion or consultation had taken place with those who would be most affected by this change – according to residents and market traders. It was a disaster. I was not the only one tripping and sliding over the prominently rounded cobbles. Pushing the

7

buggy was a trial, and rattled the baby's bones. The cobbles were hard to walk on in high heels, sandals, clogs and any shoes that were not 'sensible'. Market traders with traditional metal-rimmed wooden-wheeled carts found it difficult to manoeuvre them along the cobbles, as well as extremely noisy, waking the neighbourhood at an ungodly hour as they set up.

After a huge row, tarmac was relaid. But as we saw later, during roadworks when the road was dug up, the tarmac had been laid directly over the cobbles, rather than recycling the £1 million cobblestones. A metaphor for the times: covering expensive mistakes instead of tackling them properly is a recurring theme in this narrative.

I decided to stand for the Council after my local councillors had helped me with the housing disaster – the collapsing, damp-riddled roof – mentioned previously. Luckily for me, I had friends and local Councillors to support and advise me as to how to tackle the ridiculous bills they were sending me for the ceiling and roof repair, and was determined – as I went from solicitor to solicitor to find someone willing to take my case – that I would not give in to their bullying and incompetence. After five years of stress, including threats of eviction, the ridiculous invoices I had been sent for repairs was cancelled, repairs were finally carried out, and the housing association apologised and paid me a pitiful sum in compensation. I had won. And that is why I decided to become a local Councillor: so I could help people in my situation, who were so badly served but who didn't have the support network that had saved me.

Many years later, I was in the thick of it all as a local Councillor. I was constantly outraged by bad spending decisions and misdirected priorities. I could just state here that the Council is financially incompetent, and this statement would be challenged. But I don't have to state this; I have evidence. Remembering Mother Bun's wise advice, I have always done my utmost to read everything, so I am in a position to lay out the Council's extensive mismanagement for you as clearly as possible, using internal and external reports and my notes from Council meetings. Then you can decide the truth for yourself.

On occasion, I been dismissed by political opponents as a 'Marxist ideologue', which is ridiculous. I've never studied Marx. I'm an architectural historian more interested in post-war Modern Movement housing – which is, of course, political but hardly Marxist. It's what I'd call 'people politics': politics that works for everyone. Some of my old school friends tell me that, while I no longer subscribe to any religious observance, I'm still Catholic through and through, and that shapes my values. I'm not sure about that, but what motivates me to act on behalf of those who struggle to feed their families and pay their bills, while some of their neighbours are shovelling money into tax havens without a thought for others, is the sheer injustice of it, and the lack of understanding of what creates inequity.

I have no problem with people who have a great deal of money, as long as they came by it honestly, they pay the required amount of tax in the country in which it was earned, they treat their employees with respect, and they pay them a decent wage. We have thousands of such people in Kensington, and some of them are friends or allies. The way I see it? Paying tax at the proper rate is your membership of the human race. If everyone who avoids or evades tax decided to pay this membership fee and join the human race, the Exchequer would be far better off and could eliminate poverty – if it so wished.

Sadly, in Kensington and Chelsea – described by a senior Conservative Councillor as 'the richest borough in the universe' – there is a shocking level of inequality, including the poorest neighbourhood in the whole of London, Kensal Town next to Trellick Tower, as well as the least deprived, which is Queens Gate ward opposite Kensington Palace. The ongoing effects of the Covid-19 pandemic have exacerbated this inequality, which shames the Royal Borough. It is entirely avoidable.

You might say that RBKC is a microcosm of all that has gone wrong in our country in the recent past. I don't doubt that there are other councils across the country making similar mistakes, and I look at some examples in chapter 11, but in the context of huge wealth, the Council's actions are indefensible. Squandering funds on vanity projects while starving nurseries, youth clubs and lunch clubs for elderly people can never be justified. Chapter 1, 'The Royal Bank of Kensington and Chelsea', looks at this financial mismanagement in detail. The result of this misspending and overspending is analysed in Chapter 2, 'The Most Unequal Borough in Britain'. With reference to the 2011 Census, information taken from the Office of National Statistics, Child Poverty Action Group and Trust for London, among other sources, it lays out the specifics of inequality and deprivation in Kensington and Chelsea.

To follow this exposure of financial ineptitude, Chapter 3, 'The Sultan and Mrs Braithwaite', looks at housing inequality in the borough, and how national and local housing policy – and the ideology and actions of the Council – fails to benefit low-income families so that over the years hundreds of families have been squeezed out of the borough. Chapter 4, 'Fighting Gentrification, One Cupcake at a Time', looks at the actions of property developers and the

Council, who have worked together to raise property prices and drive low-income families out of the borough.

'The Surprise MP' (Chapter 5) follows the period before, during and immediately after I was elected the first ever Labour MP for Kensington on 9 June 2017 – after four recounts.

Chapters 6 and 7 on the Grenfell Tower disaster – 'Grenfell' and 'The Aftermath' – describe the night of the Grenfell Tower fire. They also look at the lead-up to the fire, and what happened afterwards, including damning reports written by the government-appointed Independent Grenfell Recovery Taskforce, the numerous policies adopted by the Council, and the many reviews of the background to the fire and its aftermath, including investigations on how Grenfell funding was spent.

Two months after the Grenfell Tower fire, the Notting Hill Carnival took place. Chapter 8, 'Carnival', looks briefly at the history and meaning of Carnival to local people, and how the 2017 Notting Hill Carnival was quiet, respectful, and a welcome respite for local people. Chapter 9, 'Hogwarts', looks at my thirty months in Parliament, with some personal insights and a round-up of the work I was involved in before losing my seat (by 150 votes) in December 2019.

Chapter 10, 'Consequences and Repercussions', explains what happened to many of the Council's plans for development of Council-owned residential estates and commercial properties – so many of which failed for various reasons, or were withdrawn after the Grenfell Tower fire. Finally Chapter 11, 'Compassionate Kensington', looks at our communities and how they have come together to help people affected by difficulties or disaster, such as post-Grenfell and during the pandemic.

Chapter 1

THE ROYAL BANK
OF KENSINGTON AND CHELSEA

While he may well regret it now, a senior Tory Councillor once publicly called RBKC 'the richest Council in the universe'. There are several reasons for this wealth: monetisation of sports facilities; selling off Council properties, such as care homes and residential street properties; outsourcing of numerous services to save money; a lack of funding invested where it could help residents who are struggling to support themselves; a lack of investment in managing and maintaining Council homes; making 'efficiency savings' on statutory services; cutting the cost of refurbishing Grenfell Tower. All this happened when the Council had one-third of a billion pounds in usable reserves (including cash reserves) – an amount unprecedented in any municipal council. Much of this money was not even invested if it was not immediately needed; it just sat in zero-interest and low-interest accounts. One resident calculated that this cost the Council a potential £10 million a year in lost investment income.

If you want to ensure that a Council has robust finances so it can fulfil all its statutory and legal duties, you must appoint people who know their subject and are highly competent. You bring in officers to run it who are knowledgeable and wise. You may decide to co-opt members or advisers from relevant business areas who are competent and think strategically. And you do your utmost to find Councillors to sit on scrutiny and oversight committees who will read their papers, ask questions, pursue answers, monitor outcomes, and have a thorough understanding of what they're doing.

Thus the existence of the Investment Committee of RBKC Council, which is charged with overseeing the running of the £1 billion pension fund set up for officers, Councillors, teaching staff, in-house staff, etc., which was – within their Terms of Reference – run very well. I sat on this committee for six years, the token Labour woman on a committee of up to twenty pinstripe-suited men. Some of the investments were indefensible – BAE, British American Tobacco, mining on sacred sites in India, anti-environmental activities. Some RBKC staff struggled with the Council's total lack of integrity in funding arrangements for their future pensions. I brought it up every year when the Council's Ethical Policy was 'reviewed', and even brought in ethical fund managers to explain their work in environmentally positive investment. They were labelled by one senior Tory Councillor 'snake-oil salesmen'.

They really should have listened; the snake-oil salesmen have done very well indeed.

When I joined the Investment Committee it was, I think, 89% funded. When I left – and I always took credit for this, to loud howls of laughter – it was over 100% funded. In 2020 it was 120% invested – the 'best funded' pension fund in the UK.

Setting aside for a moment my strongly felt ideological opposition to many of the investments, the mystery is: how can the pension fund be run so well, while in so many other financial areas the senior Councillors who run things are incompetent?

When I joined the Council in 2006, it took a while for me to understand the workings of the budget. There was always money to be spent on 'fun stuff', such as opera in Holland Park, endless civic receptions, and an annual garden party at Royal Hospital which could have rivalled the Buckingham Palace garden parties – all hats, medals and military bands. In 2007 the Mayor decided to upgrade the mayoral limousine, and insisted on a Bentley Continental Flying Spur whose list value was £132,000 (though we were told it 'only' cost the Council £95,000) and which did 14 miles per gallon. We were told it 'befitted the borough's Royal status'. I travelled in the Bentley once, to the funeral of a former Labour Councillor, and offered to chip in for petrol costs. No one laughed.

Paying for opera in Holland Park and garden parties were hardly the core duties of a Council; often they were blatant vanity projects. Should a local authority spend so much on fun stuff while squeezing the budget elsewhere? By 2014 food banks in the borough were struggling to get enough donations to feed people.

The Council's capital reserves were always 'healthy': in 2016/17 they reached, along with cash reserves, an extraordinary £333 million. This was achieved in ways that even some Conservative Councillors found inappropriate. In essence, revenue budgets were generously overestimated at the start of the year. Then at the end of the year, the resultant 'underspends' were sent over to the capital reserves. As one senior Tory said disparagingly at a Cabinet and Corporate Services Scrutiny meeting in October 2014: 'Revenue budgeting is a machine for generating capital reserves.' To which his colleague countered: 'More can be shaken out of that tree.' And the Town Clerk pitched in: 'If you can make a saving, you must.'

In total, between 2006 and 2010, when the new Tory government decided on a decade of austerity to 'balance the books' after the 2008 financial crash, RBKC was doing fine. Every year, millions of pounds continued to be 'underspent' in revenue budgets and were transferred to capital reserves.

This didn't just mean a few hundred thousand pounds here and there. Look at this between 2007 and 2010:

2007/8

Underspends on revenue budget:	£6.7 million
Underspends to capital reserves:	£3.8 million

2008/9

Underspends on revenue budget:	£2.7 million
Underspends to capital reserves:	£2.2 million

2009/10

Underspends on revenue budget:	£6.7 million
Underspends to capital reserves:	£5.1 million

In 2010, before austerity kicked in, RBKC had capital reserves of £158.9 million. Six years of austerity later, this amount had doubled. Due to these impressive reserves, many people called our Council 'the Royal Bank of Kensington and Chelsea'.

This practice of sending 'underspends' to capital reserves continued into the years of 'austerity' from 2010, where the Council made numerous unnecessary ideological cuts in the name of austerity, while in fact losing very little in terms of government funding.

Let's break that down. The government's plan to reduce council funding across the nation was based on a parallel plan for business rates retention, which was intended to help plug the gap where government funding was reduced, by allowing councils to retain more of the business rates that had previously been pooled between councils, then redistributed according to calculations I cannot fathom. For some councils, this was an unmitigated disaster. However, for RBKC Council, with its numerous high-value, famous shopping areas, and with its museums, bars and clubs, it was not.

While many councils approached the austerity programme with trepidation, RBKC was more than comfortable with its then c.£200 million in usable reserves. It lost a fair bit on government funding, but kept more of its business rates. Here are the figures, including the annual local government financial settlement (these are officially published sums).

YEAR	FORMULA GRANT	COUNCIL TAX FREEZE GRANT	RETAINED BUSINESS RATES
2010/11	£105.9m	–	–
2011/12	£108.2m	£1.9m	–
2012/13	£100.8m	£1.9m	–
2013/14	£69.2m	£0.78m	£44.1m
2014/15	£56.2m	£0.8m	£46.1m
2015/16	£41.2m	£0.8m	£46.1m
2016/17	£31.5m	–	£46.1m
2017/18	£22.3m	–	£46.1m
2018/19	£16.2m	–	£52.9m
2019/20	–	–	£65m
2020/21	£10.1m	–	£54.5m

So in 2010/11 the Council had £105.9 million in formula grant, and in 2020/21, the combination of reduced formula grant and retained business rates was £64.6 million. In essence, RBKC lost £41.3 million over ten years – just £4.3 million per year. In the same period, there were some spectacular revenue underspends, totalled across all business groups. These figures are taken from the annual Statements of Accounts:

2010/11	£9m
2011/12	£19.8m
2012/13	£24.3m
2013/14	£30.6m
2014/15	£23.4m
2015/16	£19m
2016/17	£13m
2017/18	£6.4m
2018/19	£9.7m
2019/20	£11.3m

Every year up to and even after Grenfell, most of these underspends were transferred into a capital expenditure reserve, which was spent on a wide variety of more or less essential projects. By my calculations, this totals £169.5 million.

Even after the first year of Covid-19, 2020/21, with a revenue overspend of £23 million shown in the Statement of Accounts of that year, the Council still had £288 million in usable reserves, giving a cheery message about how it would weather this – to the Royal Bank of K&C – minor hurdle. And still the juggernaut of spending continued, as it had during the years of austerity.

In short, it was business as usual.

Feel free to be the judge of the necessity of these projects. In 2010/11 – local elections year, purely by chance – £4.2 million of these 'underspends' were handed back to Council taxpayers as an 'efficiency bonus' of £50 per person.

In 2011/12, £24.4 million was spent on repaving Exhibition Road.

Then in 2014 – purely coincidentally, also an election year – a further £7.5 million was spent returning another 'efficiency bonus', this time of £100, to Council taxpayers, but this was only given to taxpayers who did not receive council tax benefit – in other words, to those who needed it least. Several of the wealthier residents objected, and sent their 'bonus' to local charities.

So 'efficiency bonuses' were returned to Council taxpayers while 'efficiency savings' (cuts) were made to frontline services. In the years of plenty, these 'efficiency savings' hit numerous frontline services. Many of these services served our most vulnerable residents, such as adult social care day centres, after-school clubs, holiday clubs, nurseries, lunch clubs for elders, public sports pitches, free swimming sessions, youth services, and so on. Meanwhile, an incredible £26 million was spent on upgrading offices at Kensington Town Hall, as part of the so-called 'Space Programme'. Bizarrely, this did not include any upgrades to the Great Hall and Small Hall of Kensington Town Hall Conference Centre, which was left stuck in the brown-carpeted 1970s without Wi-Fi, catering facilities or a press centre, seriously curtailing its ability to generate income.

We all know by now just how well the government's 'austerity programme' worked to pay down debt. In 2009/10 the national debt expressed as a percentage of gross domestic product (GDP) was

60%; in 2019/20, after ten years of austerity and belt-tightening, it had reached 80%. It was, of course, nonsense to equate government debt with a household budget, as Prime Minister David Cameron and Chancellor George Osborne were wont to do. Householders have a fixed income; they cannot just print money like the government can. And the Tory government was financially incompetent.

Of the £169.5 million RBKC revenue underspends, I calculate that £156.5 million was transferred back to capital reserves in this ten-year period to 2020. Every March, at the budget-setting full Council meeting, our Labour Group presented an alternative budget aligned with our priorities; the Tories always disdained and ignored it. I lost count of the number of times that various Cabinet Members for Finance snootily told Labour Councillors, 'You cannot spend capital on revenue projects; capital can only be spent once' – forgetting that it is the same money; it has just been renamed. Even the Town Clerk said in 2010, 'Money held in reserve is transferred back to revenue as the need arises.' But it never was. Yet, despite how often they told us this, there was always enough money for pet projects and vanity projects. RBKC is not a council run by successful businesspeople wishing to 'give back'. I'm not sure who imagined that Tory Councillors had the skills and expertise to set up and run businesses. Yet somehow they just couldn't stop meddling in areas that are not statutory duties of the Council.

Some projects were a bit, well, Marie Antoinette.

Let's look at Opera Holland Park.

Heaven only knows what inspired the Council to set up its own opera company: the only civic-run opera in the land. But in 1999, someone at the Council decided to take over the open-air space in Holland Park that had been offering various summertime music events for three years, and turn it over to opera. We have been stuck with it, for better or worse, ever since.

Over the years, the opera became established. It *always* lost money. For some Councillors, of course, the cachet of having opera in their back garden was irresistible and worth every penny. Every feudal state should have one! But the staff, and the sets, and the costumes, and the ambitions, grew and grew.

For those Councillors representing North Kensington and other less wealthy communities, the opera epitomised the Council's twisted aspirations. The seventeenth-century vestiges of Holland House, whose terrace the opera takes over for three months a year, suffered from such neglect that over the years two 'Building at Risk' notices were sent to RBKC from English Heritage. But the cherished opera continued to haemorrhage money.

The Council admitted to expenditure on the opera in 2001/2 of just under £1 million. The opera made an income of £817,000 – a net loss of over £105,000. But this gap grew each year. When I joined the Council in 2006, expenditure on the opera was a whopping £2 million and income £1.5 million: a loss of £500,000. By 2012/13, the net loss was just under £1 million. In times of so-called austerity, when the Council was cutting frontline services, it was indefensible to continue haemorrhaging precious funds on minority interest activities. The Cabinet Member for Finance, however, on being challenged, said this humungous annual loss was 'chicken feed'. The same year, the Council felt obliged to cut youth services by £520,000 and home care services by £950,000.

In June 2014 a coalition of local campaign groups staged a 'Mock the Opera' protest to draw attention to this ongoing outrage, with the slogan 'Stop K&C Council Squeezing our Services as they

Splash out on Sopranos'. At this point, usable reserves had reached £280 million, while cuts continued and the opera continued to lose money. Despite protests from some senior Tories, this was becoming a serious embarrassment.

The Council tried to sell the opera as a going concern, or hand over its management to Friends of Holland Park. But, unsurprisingly, there was zero interest. Even though they offered it for next to nothing, they literally couldn't give it away. So the Council eventually proposed setting it up as 'Independent Opera Holland Park', making this financial sinkhole sound like an exciting opportunity rather than an ongoing disaster. In 2015 a 'divorce settlement' was agreed: the Council pledged £5 million 'to cover losses until 2023', as well as further sums to pay for some capital works (discussed below).

From Council budget papers going back to 2001/2, I calculated that the loss the Council had made on the opera was £8,301,000. There was then the divorce settlement of £5 million, making it £13,301,000. Another £1.05 million was spent on 'structures', 'toilets' and 'contingencies'. It is devilishly difficult to separate general improvements to Holland Park from capital costs relating solely to the opera, but those I have found include money spent on seating structures, new canopies, costumes, a resident orchestra and temporary toilets. Then there was lots of work carried out on nearby pathways and flowerbeds – all this to pimp the already beautiful Holland Park for the influx of high-falutin' – or would-be high-falutin' – visitors. I found expenditure amounting to £4,941,380.

Also to be added to the mix are innumerable 'intangibles' and 'donations in kind' from the Council. Most of these will continue to be offered until 2023. Office space amounting to 2,300 sq ft has been available, free of charge, at the Council's Pembroke Road site throughout this period, to accommodate twenty-three (twenty-three!!) permanent staff. A similar-sized office in Niddry Lodge, a wing of Kensington Town Hall now let as offices, would cost £155/sq ft, but even at a more modest rate of £100/sq ft it could cost £200,000 per annum (pa). Six storage units have been available to the opera, again free. A very modest size of £100/sq ft could add up to £1,500 per month, or £18,000 pa. The free use of Holland House Terrace and facilities for three months a year has never been factored in, but a modest estimate based on other local parks would cost £100,000 pa. Multiply these sums by twenty-four years and you have a total of £7,632,000.

Total expenditure on the opera (as opposed to net losses) could therefore mean:

Revenue expenditure:	£35,806,000
'Divorce':	£5,000,000
Capital expenditure:	£4,941,380
Loss of rent:	£7,632,000

This adds up to a truly horrific £51,339,380: a sum that could have permanently eradicated poverty in World's End and North Ken if the Council only had the foresight and the will to see this.

We will look now at a less costly, but equally unjustifiable, project: Chelsea Care. In 2008 the Council decided to relaunch a dormant social care company as a local authority trading company. The idea was to provide social care services in the form of home care to the population of RBKC 'and beyond', while of course making a profit for the Council. It was very much intended to appeal to better-off older residents who needed some help around the home, but it started off by working with less wealthy, Council-supported clients. The Council's legal team used funds from the Strategic Regeneration Reserve (a £14 million Labour government fund that had never been accessed for its original purpose) to set up the business, and were careful to ensure that the Council's liability was restricted to £150,000 in the case of business failure. Chelsea Care was to be given three years to prove itself.

Chelsea Care was launched in February 2009, starting with brokerage for care and domiciliary care: quite literally, acting as an agent to bring commercial businesses into the home care and care home sectors. For the first year, it struggled to bring in any new business apart from the Council contract. In September 2010 a new Business Development Plan was created. It explained that Chelsea Care had found difficulties in getting staff, and that delays in getting staff Criminal Records Bureau (CRB) checks was slowing recruitment. They were also having problems getting further brokerage contracts. Despite having little success, they planned to extend into the private sector, offering 'practical and limited personal care . . . targeted at the elderly better-off'. Given the very limited scope of the care being offered – mostly shopping, chores and companionship – it is hard to imagine how Chelsea Care thought this could be profitable.

A month later the company was deemed, in a report to the Cabinet and Corporate Services Scrutiny Committee, to have been 'overly optimistic' in their business plan. It required an immediate investment of £100,000 and a further £100,000 in March 2011. In December 2010 the company was still experiencing financial problems. In October 2011, after a long and miserable period and various changes to management reported to the committee, Chelsea Care was liquidated.

This, of course, led to a loss of care for numerous elderly and disabled people who depended on Chelsea Care: this clear failure was a natural opening for the rampant monetisation of our most vulnerable residents.

Even though this company had failed miserably, the Council still believed the business model had potential, and it outsourced home care for all those who needed personal care at home, setting up a system that was widely criticised in the press for its exploitative nature and poor outcomes. At the time of writing, the borough has a shortfall of 1,200 home care workers, who are offered below the London Living Wage.

An investigation by the Scrutiny Committee concluded, bizarrely, that 'no market research into need was carried out' and that 'the venture was doomed to failure'. The Audit and Transparency Committee noted: 'The committee was pleased to hear . . . that key lessons had been learned and that the proposed staff mutual for youth services involved complete clarity at the start.' In short, they handed the service over to existing staff, with reduced funding.

'Complete clarity'. It should be said that the staff mutual for youth services, after struggling for some years, did not prosper or deliver a good service, and was also eventually liquidated.

No lessons had been learned.

Aside from the £300,000 'equity investment' into Chelsea Care, which was written off by the Council, it was noted that no costs had been calculated for legal advice, meetings with auditors and liquidators, costs to the business group of transferring clients back and forth, administration costs, bank charges and officer time. Some calculated that the loss to the Council was more in the region of £800,000.

But that, as we know, is 'chicken feed'.

Let us now turn to a very different kind of venture: the rebuilding of our best-known secondary school, Holland Park Comprehensive. I was very familiar with the former Holland Park School, as my own school, Sacred Heart Hammersmith, had various links to it and we had friends there. In fact, I've known students, teachers and others associated with the school since my teens, when it was known as 'the socialist Eton'. The school buildings were designed by Sir Leslie Martin, one of the architects who had designed the Royal Festival Hall. The school opened in 1958 and it was widely admired by the architectural and local community and students. However, by 2006 the school buildings were considered out of date and beyond redemption through extension and refurbishment – which would certainly have been the choice of many people, myself included.

Despite strong local objections, the Council decided to demolish the school and rebuild it from scratch. The sale of the 'southern site', which comprised most of the sports grounds, to fund the development, was also hugely controversial, but was agreed to by the majority Tory Council.

The first estimates for the school building project in 2009 came in at around £33 million. This soon grew to £40 million, then to £60 million. The final cost, after innumerable changes, was admitted to be £86 million, though some say it was probably nearer £100 million once fully equipped with designer furniture and IT. At the time the Cabinet Member for Families and Children's Services, who oversaw the project and countless overspends, cheerily stated that 'it cost nothing', because the southern playground was sold for a luxury residential development for the eye-watering sum of £120 million.

As costs grew, questions were asked, which culminated in a very detailed report to Cabinet in July 2013, much of which was confidential Part B 'for commercial confidentiality', so not available for scrutiny by the taxpaying public who had funded the school. Most of this was, however, then discussed in public at Cabinet and Corporate Services Scrutiny Committees. These public documents state: 'The construction market in 2006 was overheated, and contractors were able to be very selective.' This, the report went on to say, encouraged the Council to take over 'allocation of risk' by using the 'traditional' procurement route, which was considered to be the best way to attract contractors reluctant to take on the full risk of such a large project.

A contractor was selected, but then pulled out, at which point Council legal advisers reviewed the contract and advised that it should be re-tendered as a Design and Build contract, where the contractor essentially buys the design and constructs it, taking the greater risk. However, to avoid further delay the Council chose to ignore their own legal advice and kept to the 'traditional' contract route. In effect, the design and contracting were to be overseen in-house by the Family and Children's Services director, who had no experience whatsoever of running building contracts, let alone multi-million-pound projects. Part of this 2013 paper was titled 'Lessons Learned', in relation to an earlier project that had hit problems, relating to the St Quintin Centre for children with disabilities, which had met innumerable issues with its contractors and had cost over £800,000 more than estimated.

All good: the Council now felt it knew precisely how to avoid such problems. However, over the build period of the school there were 398 change orders to amend or improve detailed specifications, making the quantity surveyors' work almost impossible as each change added to costs.

The architects, Aedas, had, it seemed, been offered a blank cheque and had made the most of it. Chelsea Academy in Lots Road by Feilden Clegg Bradley had cost £40 million. The original estimate for Holland Park was a rather optimistic £33 million, though given the school's size, specification and number of students it would house, something up to £50 million might have been acceptable. In 2012, in Waregem, Belgium, Aedas had built a school of a similar size to Passivhaus standards – which are often costly - for around £22 million.

Holland Park Academy is the most expensive new school in the Western hemisphere. It is not the best. In November 2012 the school reopened. Disputes about so-called 'snags' – which were in fact major defects – continued. The swimming pool leaked inwards, due to an underground stream – this had been predicted by local residents. This meant that a long-term Community Use Agreement for local residents and groups to use the pool – itself a matter of huge controversy – was delayed for years: at the time of writing, it is still unresolved and the pool is out of use. The Council heard from students that the climate-controlled automatic windows were very noisy and disrupted lessons, especially on mild days, when they opened and closed repeatedly. Even worse, glass panels on the façade fell out randomly (one on a student, allegedly). The basement, which includes the lunch hall, was continually flooded by the swimming pool and stream, and badly secured stone facade panels on the outside of the building had fallen off.

In 2021, nine years after opening, the Council was still responsible for the cost of remedying long-standing defects to the school. Due to these ongoing defects, the school only had a short 'tenancy at will' lease, rather than the 125-year lease it would have had at handover, which would also have handed responsibility for repairs and maintenance over to the school.

Even though the Council had to pay for repairs and to fix defects, the school's senior management team found the money to spend £15,000 on Farrow & Ball paint and £6,000 on Jo Malone candles in 2018/19; students have said at the same time they had to share textbooks and make other economies. The headteacher Colin Hall earned £240,000 pa in 2020 – the fifth most highly paid headteacher in England. But it's an academy now. So who cares?

Controversy over the running of the school, about an alleged culture of bullying and fear, emerged in summer 2021. The Council, of course, washed their hands of it, despite having responsibility for child safeguarding. At the time of writing, a rebellion is brewing: Colin Hall has taken early retirement and a range of new management proposals are being considered.

The Exhibition Road project, launched in February 2012 before the London Olympics, was another that attracted disagreement. In 2008, Exhibition Road was not in a good state. I knew the road very well as I studied at the Royal College of Art (RCA), which has its main buildings on Kensington Road, but the Design/Architectural History course rooms were located in the Victoria & Albert Museum (V&A), half a mile down Exhibition Road. So I chalked up many miles rushing up and down the road between lectures, meetings and canteen visits. It is a traffic thoroughfare between the north and south of the borough across Hyde Park, and over to the Albert Hall, Science Museum, Natural History Museum and the V&A, with its very busy colleges including the Royal Ballet School, Royal College of Music, Royal College of Organists, Imperial College and the RCA. It was teeming with students and museum visitors. It deserved better.

As part of the Council's preparation for the 2012 London Olympics, which would bring yet more visitors to the borough, the Council decided to refurbish Exhibition Road, including the route down to South Kensington Station, which is one of the busiest stations in the Tube network, seeing more visitors than Gatwick Airport. In September 2008 the Council agreed to set aside 50% of £7.24 million for the work, hoping that Transport for London (TfL) would fund the rest. Westminster Council, whose boundary includes the northern third of Exhibition Road from Prince Consort Road up to Hyde Park, also got involved. Between 2008 and 2010, ambitions for the road grew. It was to be world-class: top architects were commissioned. Finally the Council agreed to contribute a whopping £24.4 million for its share.

The design included granite paving slabs in a criss-cross pattern, including pink granite shipped from China, and a controversial 'shared space' or 'single surface' design which lowered the pavements to road level, making a weaker distinction between road and pavement: this was supposed to slow down speeding traffic by making the road a shared space for both pedestrian and road traffic. Many people found this idea alarming, when used on a busy thoroughfare. Indeed, the originator of the shared space idea, Hans Monderman, had specifically said that it should only be used in quiet streets. Exhibition Road however, was a busy north–south thoroughfare. Numerous experts protested, but the shared space design was, of course, constructed.

The grand opening was the finishing touch to an extraordinarily expensive project, which had included £1 million that was spent on an 'Olympics Extravaganza', with a procession led by then Mayor of London Boris Johnson, a giant puppet elephant, and the Cabinet Member responsible for this fiasco parading up Exhibition Road, all looking faintly ridiculous. There was also a week-long festival that promised to turn Exhibition Road into Barcelona's Las Ramblas. But it was not Las Ramblas, which is lined with hotels, restaurants and cafes packed with visitors. When the museums shut, the street is empty and tumbleweed blows down the road. Despite every museum opening late during the week of the festival, every food vendor I spoke to had lost a great deal of money due to the lack of visitors, which was frankly predictable.

Due to the highly porous surface and fragile nature of the expensive granite, a budget of £175,000 was set aside every year for cleaning it. A further £1 million or so was budgeted for ongoing repairs, to ensure that matching granite would always be used. However, the stylish rubbish bins are always overflowing and chewing gum studs the paving. The Royal National Institute for the Blind and Guide Dogs for the Blind Association said that people with sight impairment avoid the area, as well as those using guide dogs, as they are confused by the lack of kerbs – a huge shame, given the efforts to which the museums have gone to become inclusive. In 2020 the Council spent a further £800,000 on hostile vehicle mitigation, to prevent potential terrorist attacks by car, which the single surface treatment makes the street especially vulnerable to. Some cyclists avoid the street, saying it is a traffic free-for-all and unsafe.

To go with this scheme, in 2012 'borough-wide Wi-Fi' was installed in lamp posts, and there was a huge public campaign to promote this. On closer questioning, however, I discovered that it was, indeed, 'borough-wide' but not 'borough-long'. It literally only covered Kensington High Street, Kensington Road and Exhibition Road. All in all, this was another hugely expensive venture, with very mixed results.

Leighton House Museum is another pet project for certain Council leaders.

It comes as a huge surprise to many residents of Kensington and Chelsea that the Council owns and runs Leighton House, a museum dedicated to Moroccan and Pre-Raphaelite arts. A straw poll carried out in Golborne Road – often called 'Little Morocco' due to the number of Moroccan people who live there – found not a single person who knew of its existence. Or, indeed, that they were paying for it.

This extraordinary building is the former home of artist and collector Frederic, Lord Leighton. He conceived the house as a tribute to his passion for everything Moroccan and – as a member of the Pre-Raphaelite Brotherhood – to his love for this period of painting. Leighton filled the house with art, objects and furniture reflecting his tastes. It was ultimately gifted to RBKC Council, who have kept it in its original state. It is run by the Council and Friends of Leighton House and is open to the public.

While Pre-Raphaelitism has gone in and out of fashion, it seems the museum has usually found support from leaders of the Council, despite Labour Councillors' suggestions that it should be gifted to the National Trust and run properly, as it was always losing money when run by the amateurish Council. In 2007/8 a Cabinet Member decided to 'improve' the building. Having found some original drawings showing the roof crowned with castellations or ziggurats, he decided to reinstate the scheme, despite not knowing whether or not this embellishment had been rejected by the architect as vulgar or *de trop*. This work, which was carried out in two phases, cost £2.9 million. A further phase in 2009/10 cost £3.1 million.

In 2016/17 the Council decided to extend Lord Leighton's former home. This was ostensibly to provide disabled access and extra education space, at an additional cost of £7.02 million. That's £13.02 million spent on a museum dedicated to Moroccan culture – about which Moroccan residents who have contributed to this venture through their council tax are completely unaware.

I'd like to discuss one particular Councillor's obsession with Pre-Raphaelite paintings. To some they are sublime, and there is certainly great artistry in this era. It is certainly romantic, although a modern mind might think it over-sentimental. Others see it as high-class erotica. In 2008, during the global financial crisis, the Council pursued funding for, then jointly purchased, Lord Leighton's painting *Clytie*. It cost £420,000. It is unclear at what point the Council felt it was justified in behaving like an art patron and spending hundreds of thousands of taxpayers' money on a picture of 'Clytie in her nightie', as some people called it. But it didn't stop there. In 2009/10, as austerity was approaching, the Council spent £82,798 on Leighton's *Cimabue's Celebrated Madonna* and £50,000 on *Nymphs in a Landscape* by Andrea Meldolla. The collection includes Leighton's *Crenaia, the Nymph of the Dargle,* which, I'm sorry to say, depicted a woman with no nightie on at all. Art or soft porn? *Disputa* was acquired by the Council in 2012/13, bringing the total cost to an incredible £552,798 spent on paintings, which might satisfy the aesthetic bent of some Members but seems completely inappropriate at a time of so-called austerity.

Delusions of grandeur relating to taxpayers' money has been well established in RBKC for years. I've already mentioned the Bentley Continental Flying Spur the Council bought in 2007 for £95,000 with a value of £134,000. While other councils eschewed chauffeurs and limousines and took to using cabs, this vulgarity was used for eleven years – until the Grenfell Tower fire, which was caused by inappropriate cladding, chosen by the Council in order to save £276,000, exposed it as the obscenity it was.

Another example of the 'largesse' of the Royal Bank of Kensington and Chelsea was the adoption of 'community budgeting' as part of the 'Big Society' ideology that Prime Minister Cameron was so enamoured of. In Golborne ward in 2009 we were already working on a project to support locally run businesses by attracting visitors to the area. Our project, Love Golborne, had a gorgeous website with maps, lists of businesses and a forum. We were at the same time ahead of our time, and reaching too far. Without stable funding and having to rely on volunteers, it was tough. So it was a positive when RBKC chose Love Golborne to be a pilot scheme for its community budgeting initiative. We encouraged local organisations, people and businesses to apply for funds. Some led to fantastic results, such as the annual Golborne Road Festival, where we closed the road for a day and celebrated our voluntary organisations, small businesses and local talents – for local people. It was wonderful: one year we had 2,000 visitors over the day, nearly all very local.

Other initiatives were less successful. Did we stem the tide of incomers displacing local businesses by supporting them? We did not. Golborne Road is now terminally 'cool', beyond gentrified, and countless local businesses and residents have been squeezed out by increasing rents; the very opposite of what we envisaged.

At the same time we were able to spread the funding to support local endeavours, and some were excellent. Equipping our community centre's computer room and finding good people to come in and give regular IT support to users, helping residents apply for training and improve their skills, went very well.

As the community budgeting scheme spread across the borough, with the slogan City Living, Local Life (CLLL), it was fascinating to see what some wards applied for. Since the scheme's inception, wealthier wards used their statutory £25,000 a year funding on all kinds of projects, many to 'improve' their area.

In 2020, mid-lockdown, we encouraged one of our many hot food suppliers to apply for CLLL funding, but were told that that wasn't what it was intended for. Imagine. We reminded the Tory Councillor responsible for CLLL what other wards had spent funding on: £25,000 on repairing historic walls that no one would admit to owning; repairing hitching posts; hanging baskets (one ward spent £9,000 on hanging baskets); planters; and dubious public art.

I made a little table with some highlights and put it on Twitter. In the end we got our funding for the hot food supplier. But it has to be reiterated: the Council's response as an institution was to agree funding for hitching posts in Knightsbridge – so you can tie up your horse when you pop into Harrods? – and to refuse funding for a local restaurant that was running out of money to buy food, which it planned to feed local people during lockdown.

On the morning of 22 October 2010, I heard something baffling on Radio 4. The then Tory Leader of Hammersmith & Fulham Council announced a 'tri-borough project to save £100 million' by working with RBKC and Westminster councils. This was announced after no consultation whatever, no warning, no details, no opportunity to discuss or scrutinise, out of the blue, on the news. As Deputy Leader of the Labour Group I went as soon as possible with the Labour Group Leader to discuss this with the Town Clerk. We had numerous questions, and I carefully recorded his answers.

We asked why opposition Councillors had not been informed of the media announcement, and we were told 'there is no protocol for courtesy'. We asked who knew about the confidential document announcing this plan: we were told that just the three leaders knew, and another who was the RBKC Leader's 'sounding board'. We said that a similar project at Barnet Council had ended up costing more, so when will we know if this has worked? The answer was: four years. Then we asked detailed questions about staff redundancy and pensions; the response was non-committal and vague. Our big question was: how reversible are these changes? The answer was: 'Everything is reversible.' The Town Clerk went on to explain that we would hardly notice the changes, as most would be 'backroom', but that there would be no discussion with opposition Councillors or indeed the residents, as 'the Leaders do not want it'. After more euphemisms such as 'managing demand' by 'preventative measures' and 'sharing expertise', he said that the Council was looking for 'savings of £45 million, £10 million a year for the next three years, to save frontline services'. He concluded that: 'This is only a reorganisation, if you take the glamour out of it.'

What was very clear was that much of these savings would be

achieved by middle and senior management staff losing their jobs, and by services being downgraded. When the announcement was made in October 2010, savings were estimated at £100 million. By June 2011 this had been reduced to £34 million. In February 2012, estimated savings for the coming year was just £2 million, while revenue underspends for that year were £12 million.

There was widespread cynicism about what was first called a 'Super-Council' then 'Tri-borough' then 3B. Residents, opposition Councillors, unions across all three boroughs and the press condemned the plans as poorly planned, ill-conceived and bound to fail.

In short, by cutting staff, sharing senior staff between councils and joint procurement of contracts, the plan was to save millions, work more effectively and 'future-proof' the Council's work. We were roundly put in our place in 2011 by the Cabinet Member for Family and Children's Services, who informed us: 'We are at the cutting edge of the future of what is happening.' This analysis failed to excite us at all.

It was an unmitigated disaster. As chair of the Cabinet and Corporate Services Scrutiny Committee 2012 to 2014, I saw all the contracts coming through, and some were a major cause for concern. Alarm bells first rang for a contract for BT for 'managed services', an imprecise term covering brand-new, untested software that would run all payments in and out of the Council, from parking fines to council tax, from teachers' pay and pensions to paying invoices from local businesses.

This new software was a huge concern to those of us who had not been taken in by salespeople's unsubstantiated claims. Also, rather than the councils sensibly spending in a pre-contract period, ensuring that all three councils recorded their payments in the same way, they decided to take on this non-standardised, complex system. Many felt it would be chaos. They were right.

Some teachers went unpaid. Pensions went astray. Small businesses had to chase payments, only to be told that the system said they'd been paid, when they hadn't. Council tax payments weren't registered, so bailiffs were sent to people who were 100% up to date with payments, and could prove it.

We had numerous reports of increased staff sickness due to stress, and many staff members came to Labour Councillors to tell us how the software was affecting their mental health. At around this time Labour Councillors proposed yet another motion to Council on offering the London Living Wage to all employees and contracted staff. The Cabinet Member for Finance responded thus:

> It is the role of the national government, through the social security system, to top up earnings in relation to family circumstances. There should be no sheltered public sector employment . . . it is best supported by benefits and the tax system.

It was turned down once again, with these very revealing words from a senior Tory Councillor: 'Well, I haven't looked this up, but I bet some get paid time off to get back to their countries.'

Months went by. Senior officers and Councillors continued to tell us these were teething problems. At my committee meeting every month, there was an item on the agenda relating the litany of errors. Good money was sent after bad. Early problems came to a head when attempts were made to combine adult social care services across the three boroughs, discussed in depth at a full Council meeting in June 2012. Records were not only incomplete, but since they were recorded in different ways in each Council, any kind of reconciliation was almost impossible. Council officers working in the same jobs were on different pay scales across the boroughs, creating friction. There was little strategic oversight, and no experts in place to deal with this kind of amalgamation. It was a mess – and it had been entirely predictable.

The official launch of 3B was in October 2012. The Council stated that the project would 'save taxpayers £80 million a year' (not £100 million, then). The then RBKC Leader was lionised across local and national government for his exciting initiative.

By March 2013 the new managed services contract from BT was still having 'teething problems'. I had thought, and the Cabinet and Corporate Services Scrutiny Committee did too, that buying new and untried software to track all our payments – every penny coming in or out of the Council – was a huge risk. Our serious concerns were minuted. It was discussed at the Audit and Transparency Committee meetings. It had been estimated to save £13 million across all three boroughs, but had not been sufficiently resourced to deliver anything like these savings, and new staff had to be taken on to manually track every payment and input data that should have been transferred automatically. This was recorded in committee papers as a 'disappointment'.

By April 2013 there was a 'limited assurance' report to the Audit and Transparency Committee on BT's work, meaning that Council auditors considered the BT contract to be a risk that needed to be fully scrutinised. Much of the blame went to Westminster Council, which was running the contract. Even after the extra teams had been employed to deal with the errors and lost payments, and further money had been paid to BT to get it right, problems continued. The system failed to collect income, and failed to reconcile when it had been paid, leading to contractors and employees going unpaid, sometimes for months, undermining their business, and residents being chased for bills they had paid. The councils continued to send bailiffs out to collect supposedly unpaid bills, which was not only appalling but terrifying for residents targeted unfairly.

Teachers were still not being paid, pensioners were not being paid, and at one point nearly £27 million could not be reconciled – it was actually missing from the accounts for some months. The Council admitted that they had lost £10 million on the BT contract. Heaven only knows about the rest, as the losses were closely guarded.

In April 2017, the Council finally decided to withdraw from the 3B arrangements – at vast expense. The councils then had to pursue BT through the courts for compensation. At the time of writing this is still dragging through the legal process.

After so many poorly managed contracts, in February 2015 a colleague who had taken over from me as chair of Cabinet and Corporate Services Scrutiny Committee set up a cross-party Working Group to scrutinise procurement practice in the Council. It was very clear that the Tory leadership was not at all keen for this to take place, but in the end they reluctantly accepted it. Working Groups are cross-party committees that investigate specific issues over an agreed period of time: they then report back to the overarching committee, in this case the Cabinet and Corporate Services Scrutiny Committee. I was happy to serve on this Working Group. Our chair was a methodical contract lawyer with suitable expertise

– for once. We looked forensically at sixteen projects that had caused long-term problems for the Council. We were tasked with finding out what had gone wrong, so the Council could improve its commissioning and procurement practice and avoid the same problems cropping up in the future.

Among the projects put under the microscope were Holland Park Academy and BT managed services, both discussed earlier. Then there was Amey's contract for facilities management (now ended after endless problems) and the reorganised 3B arrangements for adult social care, both of which had received a 'limited assurance' report at the Audit and Transparency Committee.

One of the most alarming failures, due to the vulnerability of those involved, was that of Special Educational Needs (SEN) Transport, the contract that provided transport for our most vulnerable children and adults, taking them to school and back home, or to day care or hospital appointments. The Council recontracted, to save money, and found a cheaper supplier. This did not start well. There were a series of problems that risked children's well-being and put them in potential danger. After protests from some elected representatives, I'm sorry to report that a senior officer, challenged about the potential dangers of this service, said 'These children have been treated like royalty for too long.'

We had an emergency Council debate in an attempt to persuade those in power in the Cabinet to take this seriously. The 'sovereign standard' from pick-up to drop-off was fifty-five minutes maximum; for a vulnerable person with potentially multiple physical issues, this has to be the limit. Instead, journeys were lasting up to an hour and twenty minutes. Staff picked children up late from home and delivered their charges at school late and distressed. Staff accompanying children should have had CRB checks and training to care for people with multiple needs; many had neither. All staff were to have up-to-date information on their charges' complex needs; many had no more than a list of names. All staff were to be on PAYE; many were self-employed or even paid cash so were not on the books and were therefore unaccountable. It was a classic downgrading of services to save money. It did not.

This new contract had disastrous results. Some minibuses did not have the correct seatbelts or harnesses fitted so children were able to remove them, putting them in danger. One child arrived so late at school that they had soiled themselves. Another day the staff did not have the correct home address for a child who was non-verbal, and literally took the child from house to house asking if the child lived there. One child became so anxious that they had a fit and were admitted to hospital; the parents feared the child could have died.

Eventually the Council ended this new contract. One senior officer complained to a Labour Councillor that the new contract was 'costing more now, and I hope you're satisfied'.

The cross-party report on Procurement Scrutiny was complex and detailed, but was finally ready for publication at the end of 2015. However, the Council was determined to study it in advance of publication so that they could formulate a 'response' – clearly to minimise its impact and reach. It was finally published in September 2016. The Council then refused to allow a debate on it at a full Council meeting, but in their formal response to Cabinet they roundly denied many of the report's findings and recommendations, stated that they were already implementing many of the others, and grudgingly accepted some others. The

Council's response was typical: delay the response, minimise the findings, deny much of it, then fix a few ongoing issues behind the scenes. Reputation is all.

By April 2017 it was public knowledge that the six-year 3B experiment had failed. The Leader of RBKC Council said in *K&C Weekly News* that the cost of ending the tri-borough deal 'is likely to be in the millions'. RBKC and Westminster Council were at pains to blame the then Labour-led Hammersmith & Fulham Council. Their formal statement said: 'Since its creation, the tri-borough project has been credited with improving services while realising significant savings.'

One of the Council's numerous projects at the time was the building of the new school and leisure centre at Lancaster Green and the subsequent refurbishment of Grenfell Tower, via a web of contracts and subcontracts that meant – as we heard at the Grenfell Public Inquiry – it was almost impossible to determine accountability. During the long and tortuous process of contracting, it was finally determined that it was best for the Council to retain project management; lessons had been learned and they had the experience to do it. It opened in September 2014.

Just two and a half years later, on 14 June 2017, metres from the new school, was the fatal fire at Grenfell Tower, in which seventy-two people died.

The 'Royal Bank of Kensington and Chelsea' was a busted flush. The Council's constant failure to manage contracts – masked by once huge reserves – has never resulted in the 'lessons learned' that have so often been quoted. Consequences of these misdirected priorities reach far and wide. The Council is not a corporation; it is a local authority bound legally and morally by statutory duties.

And many people would say that the Council has failed to meet these duties.

The inevitable, tragic consequences of years of spending priorities moulded by the 'Royal Bank of Kensington and Chelsea' are there for all to see: the avoidable atrocity of Grenfell, and the appalling reality of our beautiful borough being 'the most unequal borough in Britain'.

Chapter 2

THE MOST UNEQUAL BOROUGH
IN BRITAIN

I often tell people that the best way to enter national politics is to start as a local councillor. More than anything, this is a trial of character: a grounding in persistence and in finding hidden horrors in 200-page reports. If you are caring and strong enough to serve a couple of terms as a local councillor, with all its frustrations, the need for determination and candour, knowing where to go for support, dealing alone with the details of complex casework, working with a team of opinionated colleagues, learning what you can and cannot do within the rules you must get to grips with, from speaking in public and dealing with the press to leafletting, canvassing and sometimes getting yelled at by members of the public – if you can deal with all that, then you are reasonably qualified to enter parliament. You will also be a valued contributor in Select Committees.

If indeed that is your ambition. It isn't for everyone.

A life in politics shouldn't really be attractive to people with nothing to offer but personal ambition. If you are a councillor, your ambitions should be for others. Sometimes people will say to me, 'Oh, you work for the Council, don't you?' And I say, 'No, I work for you, and the Council works for me. At least, that's how it's supposed to work.' The role of public servants is to serve their electorate.

Of course, there are battalions of 'self-servatives' of all political persuasions who blithely ignore the above advice and achieve Council Cabinet or government ministerial posts with few qualifications apart from a few million in the bank from property deals, a brief career in finance, unquestioning self-belief allied with unqualified ambition, a generous redundancy payment, or possibly all of the above. Perhaps some of these people aren't the kind of people we would wish to serve us in government. They support our somewhat feudal system, and believe that because they are so numerous that they don't need to listen to disaffected voters, that they are unimpeachable. However, merely having a majority does not always mean that you represent the best intelligence, competence, knowledge or indeed caring. Ideally, candidates for elected positions would understand their skills and their limits, and would appoint people to work with them who fill the gaps in their expertise.

So if you don't learn new ways of thinking and have your eyes and heart opened as you serve at the coal face, you end up taking your preconceptions, ignorance and entitlement with you onto the national stage of parliament. But you will be in danger of becoming a narrow-minded, unquestioning, obedient, possibly racist, possibly snobbish and uncaring member of a dispassionate elite – in local or national government. And we will all be the poorer for it.

And here we are.

Living in the community I serve, I thought I was well aware of the difficulties people face. Indeed, I have faced quite a few myself. When women come to my surgery with a baby in a buggy that's stacked with lever-arch files documenting a long campaign of attrition against them by their landlord, I often think, 'I was that woman once'. When you become a councillor, you become much closer to the people you serve. As they get to know and trust you, they let you into their lives, and they may be far worse off than you could ever have imagined.

When I was elected to the Council in 2006, it was at a time of relative economic stability. Under a Labour government we had child tax credits, working tax credits and Sure Start nursery provision, all of which I relied on at times. It was just about possible to work part-time, care for young children, and put food on the table. As a single parent of three children, I would certainly have found it difficult to survive without the Labour government's tax credit system.

The financial crash of 2008 reduced the number and quality of part-time jobs available, and the election of a Tory government in 2010 – a government of Eton boys with inherited wealth or wealth made in the City – contributed to a deadly downturn for many families who had previously been managing their finances and their lives.

As the benefit system grew more punitive and miserly, I began to see far more cases of alarming hardship. I heard from a local dentist that more and more primary-age children were having teeth extracted – not due to decay, but to malnutrition. A GP told me that some children were starting nursery visibly undersized, most likely due to malnutrition in the womb. This played on my mind endlessly. Where possible, when I did a home visit, I would ask the mother if she minded me looking in her kitchen cupboards. What I saw could be disturbing. In a home that was kept clean and tidy, with children who were well behaved and nicely dressed, one day I found two tins and a bag of pasta in the kitchen cupboard – and that was it for a family of three for the next five days. I met some women who were spending their money on feeding their children and eating their leftovers – if there were any. If not, they drank tea to fill their bellies. Two women, I will never forget. They were stick-thin. They were starving themselves to feed their children. This was in 2012, in the Royal Borough of Kensington and Chelsea.

Things have, of course, got worse since then. So much worse.

In one case a family who needed to move due to overcrowding had been told that they would be considered for a move once they had paid off rent arrears accrued during a period of illness. They were so desperate to move that they were paying far more than they could afford. I was angry about this, as I knew that the chance of them being moved was very low. I invited the housing officer to a meeting and put her on the spot. 'Once they've paid the arrears, realistically, what are their chances of being rehoused?' I asked. It was, as I feared, next to zero. We rearranged the repayments so the family could afford to eat a little more. It took ten years to get them moved. *Ten*.

As so often happens in these cases, housing officers make the lives of those who are struggling much worse. I was lucky to find an officer who was honest enough to admit that the punitive repayment system she had set up was unlikely to get the family any kind of respite from overcrowding. Many housing officers treat their tenants with disdain. In the old days of housing associations, people like me would have worked for them. But over the years their 'mission' has changed dramatically, from providing low-cost housing for people on a low income to being property developers. Staff are often poorly trained and poorly paid, badly treated and overworked, and lack any kind of empathy. Instead, they police their tenants, who often fear them. I tell people: 'Remember, they work for you. You are paying their wages.' But that doesn't help.

In 2013 a Councillor colleague put a motion to the Council on children's health, stating that 'hunger is a public health emergency'. The roar of disbelief from the Tories at the mention of food poverty was extraordinary. A Tory Councillor who ended up being the MP before me stated that work on addiction had a far higher priority, and that the Council was fulfilling its obligations. Another, destined to be Leader of the Council, stated, wide-eyed, that vulnerable families get visits from health visitors. Both comments were utter nonsense. I had carried out some research and found that in the past three years across Hammersmith & Fulham, Kensington and Chelsea, and Westminster, there had been sixty-five hospital admissions for hypocalcaemia – Vitamin D deficiency– and a shocking ten emergency admissions for such severe hypocalcaemia that the person had gone into shock and collapsed, unconscious. Inevitably, many were older people, but some, disturbingly, were children. I said that if this continued, we would have a re-emergence of rickets. The other Cabinet Members disbelieved us. The Cabinet Member for Family and Children's Services shouted mockingly, 'Labour love the idea of rickets!'

That was 2013. In 2020 a child was diagnosed with rickets, an incurable lifelong condition, in North Ken. It sickens me that this was predicted, and avoidable.

Determined to prove my point, and with local elections on the horizon in 2014, I submerged myself for two weeks in the Office of National Statistics (ONS) neighbourhood statistics website. At that time – sadly no longer, as it ended in 2017 – it gave detailed analysis of statistics from 'lower super-output areas', which are groups of around 500 households. Today you have to pick through the stats and do the analysis yourself, which is time-consuming but a very valuable exercise. This level of detail is essential when researching inequality. Otherwise you just find meaningless averages.

Let me explain.

The average life expectancy across Kensington and Chelsea is the highest in the UK. Great news! In the lower super-output area around Harrods, for a white British-born man in 2013, this was the spectacular age of ninety-two. Amazing! However, in Golborne ward, in the lower super-output area of Wornington Green, a Catalyst Housing estate for social tenants, the average life expectancy for a Moroccan man was sixty-two. That's a shocking thirty-year difference between the wealthiest and most deprived areas, within a twenty-minute bus ride.

I've been 'corrected' countless times on this. I've been told that the difference in life expectancy between North and South Kensington is six years, eighteen years, lots of different calculations, but as I say, in such an unequal borough, how averages are calculated render this meaningless. Nonetheless, the government felt justified, after looking at these meaningless averages, to raise the pension age 'as we are all living longer'. Well, 'we' may be, but our neighbours may never make it to pension age. 'We' may be living into our nineties off the sweat of our neighbours' backs.

As I was deep in research one night, I had a brainwave. Could

Kensington and Chelsea be 'the most unequal borough in Britain'? I delved deeper into the ONS neighbourhood statistics to find out. They were so much worse than I imagined.

In 2013 Kensington and Chelsea was indeed 'the most unequal borough in Britain'. It has actually got worse since then, but more of that later. Child poverty across London averages 28%; the average in 'the richest borough in the universe' is 27% – nothing to crow about. However, in some areas of the borough it is a shocking 57%.

Here is a snapshot of the situation from detailed research done in 2013, taken from the ONS neighbourhood statistics. In Queen's Gate ward, opposite Kensington Palace, child poverty was 2.8%. In Henry Dickens Court, Notting Dale ward (where Grenfell Tower is located) it was a disgraceful 57.6% – worse than the Gorbals in Glasgow, at 49.7%.

The Child Poverty Action Group estimate that each child living in poverty costs the economy £10,000 a year. In Kensington and Chelsea in 2013, there were 5,250 children living in poverty. That's costing the economy over £52 million a year. I'll leave that thought with you.

We've looked at life expectancy and the extraordinary gap between income groups in the borough, but it isn't just a north versus south situation. There are places where your life expectancy can drop by ten years just by crossing a road. That's because in many areas mixed communities live cheek by jowl. Of course, most of us like that, but the unfairness sticks in the throat. 'Health inequality' is scored in various ways. K&C is ranked first in England and Wales for self-assessed health as 'very good' (at 57.8%, compared to an average of 50% across London). But that is made up of a mixture of smaller neighbourhood areas of, for example, 0% health deprivation in Beaufort Gardens off Knightsbridge, and an appalling 65% in Henry Dickens Court.

Income inequality is another interesting indicator, and this is where the calculation of averages needs to be clearly defined. In 2013 household median income (adding everything together and dividing by half) in K&C was £101,000, the highest in the country. However, the mean average income (the one you would get if you lined everyone up in the borough in order of their salary and asked the person in the exact middle of the line what they earned) was £36,000, and a third of all workers, the majority of them in North Kensington, earned below £20,000. At that time the mean average income in the World's End council estate in Chelsea was £13,125, whereas if you crossed King's Road to the lovely Victorian terraces of the 'Ten Acres' around Hobury Street, the average would be £100,000.

In May 2006 Ken Livingstone pledged commitment to a London Living Wage for workers in the capital. In May 2009 Mayor Boris Johnson, at Mayor's Question Time, following on from his predecessor's pledge on the London Living Wage, said:

> During these testing times it is vital that we invest in order to pay Londoners a fair and decent wage. A London Living Wage is not just morally right but it makes commercial sense, as all businesses need good, willing and motivated workers to support them through the recession and on to greater prosperity when the upturn comes. It also brings wider social benefits, tackling poverty, making work pay, and improving the quality of life for families.

We put motions to Council in 2010 and 2011 on adopting the London Living Wage for all Council employees and contractors' employees. We had a lot of opposition. I worked out that in 2011, a job of forty hours a week at minimum wage would pay around £13,000 a year – just a little over a backbench Councillor's allowance. So, as I put it, 'What is pin money for some Councillors is poverty pay for low-income workers.' Our motion was met by Tory outrage. The Cabinet Member for Finance responded to our motion in the local paper:

> It is the role of the national government through the social security system to top up earnings in relation to family circumstances. Moreover, if the Council and its contractors did adopt the London Living Wage, it could add anything up to £1 million to the Council's costs, equivalent to a 1% increase in council tax, increasing the household bills of many low-income families not working in local government.

As we saw earlier, £1 million a year was pretty much the annual net cost to the Council of subsidising the loss-making opera in Holland Park. And there's also the cost of adding to the art collection at Leighton House. For the record, I wouldn't mind at all about the Council subsidising minority-interest arts if some of my full-time working neighbours weren't starving themselves to feed their children. This failure in their duty of care is a constant concern to me.

Another of the indicators of inequality is living conditions. Poorly maintained social housing is rife: a quick search on Twitter will confirm this, with photos. Overcrowding is widespread, especially in social housing. Of course K&C is a densely populated borough, but that is on the basis of built density (how many homes and bed spaces), rather than lived density (how many people live there permanently). It is always interesting to look at the number of second and empty homes alongside density and overcrowding. In 2013 there were 1,200 long-term empty homes and 9,300 second homes in K&C, and this has remained fairly constant over the years since. If you add the number of Airbnbs and other short-term let homes registered in 2017 (3,476), that means just under 14,000 homes (15%) in K&C are not lived in permanently.

In Golborne ward in North Kensington, 63% of families are overcrowded. In Campden ward, around Kensington Town Hall, just 18% are overcrowded. How this is measured may give you an idea of the reality of overcrowding. It is simply based on sex and age, and what the Council sees as reasonable for two children sharing a room, which is based on age. However, these statistics hide a wide range of issues. I've spoken to families where young children had to share a double bed with their parents or their granny: in one case, this was a ten-year-old boy. I've seen a bedroom with five mattresses on the floor for the children, as there was not enough room for beds; a room where four children slept in bunks, including two teenagers of the opposite sex, where they had to take turns doing homework, going to bed, getting dressed; a room where a girl studying for her GCSEs had to wait for her family to go to sleep so she could study on the stairs, as she shared a bedroom with two siblings and her parents slept on the sitting-room sofa.

Of course, this kind of overcrowding isn't just an inconvenience. Sleep is scarce and of poor quality when so many people share a room. Often damp builds up, leading to asthma, and the steroids that treat asthma slow down growth. Of course, doing homework becomes a near impossibility, which is one of many reasons that homework clubs – at times much derided as 'unnecessary' by the Council – are a real life-saver for so many children, as well as a place of safety for children whose homes feel chaotic or who can't go home until their parents return from work.

The problem of people not having enough space persists outside as well. The Royal Borough of Kensington and Chelsea is blessed with parks and green spaces, tennis courts and other sporting facilities. However, over the years these have been monetised, with former kickabout spaces either developed or turned into 'booking only' facilities where you must book and pay a fee in advance. Today there are few parks where you can take a football and set up a casual game of footie with whoever is around.

One of the most notorious cases is that of the sports pitches at Lancaster Green on the Lancaster West estate. Lancaster West and Grenfell Tower were built to replace an area of 'slum' housing, and Lancaster Green was the green space afforded to the estate as its lungs and leisure space. (A little history here. Before Lancaster West and the Tower were built in 1972, there was a public baths and swimming pool on the site, built in 1878. At the time, the baths were a saviour to many. One resident told me that they held regular swimming sessions that cost 1d (a penny). Many of the boys who went had no swimming trunks, so swam naked, and these swimming sessions went down in history as the 'penny bums'.)

Labour Councillors whose constituents couldn't get their children into schools in the borough had demanded for many years that a new secondary school should be built. The Council insisted there was no need for another school, but eventually – and by then it was totally their own idea, of course – they decided that a new school was needed. We hunted high and low for the best location, but the Council was set on building on Lancaster Green. This green and its sports pitches were all the amenity space the residents of 795 homes on the Lancaster West estate had, so at least 2000 residents. Residents quite rightly complained that losing this essential facility would disadvantage them. There was an almighty row on numerous fronts. But the Leader of the Council wouldn't budge, saying finally: 'Take this school where we say, or dump it.'

Early concerns were simply for loss of leisure space, but concerns grew around the sports pitch being relocated. It was used by local clubs and groups but otherwise available for residents' use. The plan to 'move' it to form part of Westway Sports Centre, next to the West Cross Route and the Westway, was not welcomed. First, it was several minutes' walk from the previous site, which meant that younger children would not be able to use it without supervision. Second, there would be a charge to use it, and it would have to be booked in advance. Third, and worst of all, the location was in one of the most polluted spots in the borough, literally underneath a busy motorway. During a very heated Planning meeting, a Tory Councillor – who, by chance, was an oncologist – and I made the Council agree to monitor air pollution in the area before it started work. This was agreed. But in the end the Cabinet Member responsible for implementing this commitment did not participate. Local residents were disgusted and alarmed, and undertook some 'guerrilla air monitoring' using kits from King's College where London-wide air quality monitoring takes place. The results were appalling. Needless to say, the sports pitch was built there, in a pollution hotspot, and young people are put at risk every day, gulping down filthy air as they exercise.

One of the longer-term outcomes of this monetisation of sports pitches that were previously free of charge is the rising levels of obesity in primary school children. In 2013 we had another extraordinary debate in Council on tackling childhood obesity, when the government had offered the Council funding to address this problem.

Labour Councillors proposed bringing back free swimming for school-age children, which had been stopped a couple of years previously, and freeing up sports pitches at certain times so children could play at will. Since funding for school sports had also been decimated, it was no surprise to us that this had had an effect on children's health. Also, perhaps more controversially, I suggested that when times are hard and time and money are in short supply, parents rely on cheap food to fill small bellies. 'That's why mums go to Iceland,' I said, copying a popular TV ad of the time.

The then Leader of the Council wouldn't have it. 'I know why children are putting on weight,' he drawled. 'When parents take their children to farmers' markets, the children constantly beg for a bit of this and a bit of that. Parents must learn to say no.'

His disconnect from reality was disturbing. You can feed a family of four with cheap food from Iceland for £2 or £3. One snack from a farmer's market can set you back £6. What world was he living in?

At that time, around 1,000 of our children were living in bed and breakfast or temporary accommodation, sometimes a significant distance from their school and local networks. Did they have the time or money to enjoy sports? In 2020, the number of children in B&B or temporary accommodation (TA) had risen to 1,800.

Another shameful area of inequality is how we accommodate and care for our elderly people. This is a borough where 300 Chelsea Pensioners (army veterans aged over 65) live in the splendid Christopher Wren-designed quarters at Royal Hospital near Sloane Square. This is the degree of care and respect we would like all our older residents to experience if they need care at home or residential care.

Failing that, our elders should at least receive the degree of care and attention we would like to receive ourselves, if and when we need it. However, in this borough, which has more than 20,000 over-65s, with a growing number of people living into their eighties and nineties (at least in some areas), the Council has seen fit to dispose of every single one of its residential care homes where elders who need constant care can be safely accommodated. Between 2006 and 2009 there was a huge battle over Edenham Residential Care Home in Golborne ward, which formed part of Ernö Goldfinger's 'cradle to grave' complex of buildings, which includes Trellick Tower. This was my first heartbreaking campaign after joining the Council.

In 2006 the Council decided that 'due to demographic change' residential care was soon to be entirely obsolete. We didn't believe it, but at that point we had no statistics to contradict them. Their proposal went hand in hand with a decision to move all forty-seven residents of Edenham Residential Care Home and demolish it, as it was no longer 'fit for purpose'. This was the first time I had heard this term, and it disturbed me. With my background in Modern Movement architectural history, and colleagues who had actually worked with Ernö Goldfinger, I knew it to be inaccurate.

Edenham Residential Care Home had been designed as a

two-storey-tall and -wide T-shaped structural shell, with interior spaces and divisions that were non-structural. It had been carefully designed to be flexible. Goldfinger had designed a 'future-proof' building.

The Council, of course, would not listen. They had made their decision using their large majority and were intent on finding 'evidence' to support it. 'Decision-based evidence-making', as they call it in the trade.

We ran a huge campaign including all residents who were able to get involved (many had dementia), relatives and local people to try and save this local service. We brought in legal advisers who signed up as clients a number of residents, including an entirely cogent ninety-three-year-old. The Council were furious: not for the first time we were treated as 'rogue Councillors'. They demanded that staff inform them if I, or any other Councillors or campaigners arrived at the home to support our residents. This was in our ward! We had a perfect right to represent these vulnerable elders and their families. We had known some of the residents for years: they were the elders of large North Ken dynasties. In the end we worked out that it took officers around forty minutes to get there after they'd been notified. From then on, whenever we went round, we worked quickly, though I nearly got caught one day and had to hide in the toilets.

Tony Benn came in one day to support us. He came in an hour before the press and TV crew arrived to speak to residents – a characteristically considerate approach. He wanted to hear first-hand from residents and family members, and to work out who might be happy to go public.

But all this was to no avail, and the Council started to move out the forty-seven residents. It was heartbreaking. Dementia affects people in very different ways. Some people who have been easy-going and charming their whole lives become difficult, verbally abusive, even physically violent. For others it's the opposite. I well remember my Spanish granny, who nearly made it to one hundred, treating every day as a party and us all as her guests, even though she didn't recognise any of us towards the end.

It's not like that for everyone. One dementia sufferer didn't like his new home a few streets away: he used to escape and try to return to Edenham, in bare feet and pyjamas, buzzing to be let in. Another who was moved out of the borough would wander the streets for hours, looking for Edenham. One was lost for several days, and was eventually found in a North London hospital, having no idea who they were. I visited some in their new places. One man refused to let anyone he didn't know touch him. He was filthy and unkempt, with fingernails like claws. An African-Caribbean woman was moved to a home run mainly by East European care workers. Kind as they were, they had never been shown how to care for her hair, which quickly became matted. Many people declined quickly, which is not unusual for patients with dementia when they are moved to unfamiliar places. In the year after Edenham closed, twenty-one of its residents died. There were endless funerals.

Two elderly men with severe dementia simply refused to eat and died of starvation. One, whose family I knew well, was a lovely, courteous person, even when severely ill. I visited him in hospital three days before he died. He beckoned me over and whispered in my ear, so his daughter couldn't hear, 'You can tuck me in any time.' This was William Rogers who, along with his family, was a stalwart of the campaign. We committed to name the building we in the community were planning to replace Edenham the William Rogers Health Centre in his memory, and to commemorate all those who died before their time due to bad Council decision-making.

The care home was finally vacated and the staff brutally moved elsewhere at a lower pay scale, or made redundant. Then the Council moved to demolish the building: the only residential care home Ernö Goldfinger had ever designed. One rainy day a group of us went over to protest, and I chained myself to the gates. We got a lot of press attention, but ultimately the Council got its way and the building was demolished. But to what end? Ten years and countless unnecessary deaths later, the site is still a temporary car park. And lo and behold, the Council has decided that 'due to demographic change' we need more residential care. But, of course, not in the borough. This makes it almost impossible and costly for relatives to visit their elders, moved to less expensive boroughs in the capital, who quickly decline. So, while the last Council-run site for residential care in Chelsea was sold off to a provider of what I have called 'caviar care' for the super-rich, we are witnessing what I call 'social cleansing of the elderly'.

Meanwhile, the project to keep people in their own homes by providing home care has been derailed by the creeping failures of home care providers, which are often owned by hedge funds and equity funds, creaming off profit and letting them fail when it suits them.

Armed with all these examples and statistics, in 2014 I launched my 'most unequal borough in Britain' campaign in the run-up to the local elections. We published stats in different subject areas each day leading up to polling day. I can't pretend it had the immediate impact I had hoped for, but the cumulative impact over time was very satisfying. A journalist for the *Independent* dedicated a full-page article to the 'Walk of Shame' from South Ken to North Ken. A course on Public Health at Canterbury University dedicated a module to the same issue, and the course lecturer visited me two or three times with his students. And 'the most unequal borough in Britain' description stuck.

In March 2017 we put another motion to the Council about the prevalence of food banks in the borough. A Cabinet Member responded thus: 'The real danger is not lack of food but the wrong food . . . [nutritional education] is a better place to spend public money.'

The Leader of the Council accused us of 'cheap sloganising', and in a subsequent column in the local paper was even more out of touch: 'There was a veritable orgy of virtue signalling when the subject of food banks came up in debate . . . food banks are making a welcome and important contribution to our welfare arrangements. Food banks are a fine and noble thing.' In September of the same year, multi-millionaire MP and alleged tax avoider Jacob Rees-Mogg said on the expansion of food banks that it was 'rather uplifting' and 'shows what a compassionate country we are'.

In his column in May 2017, the Leader of the Council was fulsome in his praise for a recent prosecution of a private landlord due to serious safety concerns: 'There are some bad apples who put tenants at risk by flouting safety standards . . . any landlords who fail to meet their obligations will face prosecution.'

Two weeks later the Grenfell Tower fire killed seventy-two people. It was entirely preventable.

Needless to say, the Council Leader did not deliver himself to the authorities to face prosecution.

In November 2017 I published a further report 'After Grenfell: Housing and Inequality in Kensington and Chelsea: The most unequal borough in Britain'. This was an evidence-based report looking at housing statistics published by numerous organisations and charities, with a 'state of affairs' update on Grenfell rehousing, along with some of the issues that were being faced at the time by our Grenfell homeless. Just after the fire, Prime Minister Theresa May committed to rehouse everyone 'within three weeks': nearly six months later, only twenty households had been rehoused. More broadly, I found that 4,500 children were living in poverty in the Royal Borough, and according to the Child Poverty Action Group (CPAG) this cost the taxpayer *c.*£49 million. Child obesity – another result of poverty – had doubled over the same period, as had hip fractures among the over-65s (hip fractures are often a sign of osteoporosis). Diabetes in K&C had doubled since 2010, and life expectancy had dropped by six years.

It was not a flattering picture.

I was roundly and publicly berated for it by the Leader of the Council thus:

> Using the Grenfell disaster to try and drive a wedge between communities in the borough is just opportunistic. This report, littered with typos [it wasn't] and factual errors [it was referenced, so no], only tells us some of the things we know already and want to tackle in the coming years under the Council's new leadership.

A lobbying firm, allegedly spurred on by No. 10 Downing Street, carried out a 'hit job' on me for saying something critical about a Tory parliamentary candidate that a former friend of his had told me – ten years previously. A classic dogpile to drown out the unwelcome truth of my report.

The above comment from the Leader of the Council was an unfortunate baseline from them; they should have learned by then that I keep a record of all their statements.

A further report on inequalities written by me during lockdown in October 2020 revealed that inequality in the borough had worsened dramatically, before taking Covid into account, and that the area around Grenfell Tower, which had received tens of millions of pounds from both government and the Council, had in fact got poorer. This time the Council's response was a deafening silence.

'The most unequal borough in Britain – revisited' reprinted the 2014 report, along with fourteen pages of even more highly detailed and updated statistics from 2020. Without including any changes that were due to the pandemic, child poverty averaged across the borough had worsened, at 38%, and the infant mortality rate of 3.4% was among the worst in London, second only to Barking and Dagenham. The uptake rate for the MMR vaccine, which protects against measles, mumps and rubella, is not far from the lowest in the country, at 76.1%, and as this is a borough average, in some areas this will be even lower. Conversely, there are likely to be areas where it is much lower – vaccine hesitancy is likely to have contributed to the rate of deaths and long Covid in the borough. Though it is too early to define this, just two-thirds of North Kensington adults were fully vaccinated against Covid in spring 2022. Dental health in children was also worse than the average across the country, with 26.6% of children experiencing untimely loose teeth, decay and tooth extraction.

Life expectancy, shockingly, had dropped by six years in Kensal Town in North Kensington since 2010. This decrease was the worst in the country and was picked up by Professor Sir Michael Marmot in his updated Marmot Report of February 2020. According to the Index of Multiple Deprivation, Kensal Town in Golborne ward scored a shocking 59%, worse than Stonebridge Park in Brent, which has always been known for widespread deprivation. Of the five lower super-output areas in Golborne ward, two were in the most deprived 5% in England. Meanwhile, Chelsea Manor in Royal Hospital ward, Chelsea, had a 7.6% deprivation rate, one of the least deprived in the country.

Health inequality had also worsened: 61% of residents in World's End estate in west Chelsea reported suffering long-term ill health, whereas just eleven bus stops down the King's Road in Hans Town, just north of Sloane Square, had an impressive −3.2% health deprivation rate, among the best in the country (the minus figure is due to the excellent health in the area surpassing normal measures). The same sad story applied to income inequality, employment, living conditions and educational attainment. Worst of all was that in K&C we had the three *most* deprived and the three *least* deprived wards in London: for the first time, Notting Dale ward, where the Grenfell Tower fire occurred in 2017, was among the most income-deprived in London, which may have come as a surprise to those who have watched as tens of millions of pounds have been spent in the area.

But perhaps we shouldn't mind. As one Tory Councillor told me: 'You can spoil a child with too much education and health.'

So much for the reports I wrote, which were treated with disdain and sometimes mocked, even though I referenced the Office of National Statistics, Trussell Trust, Trust for London, CPAG, etc. In November 2021 the highly regarded charity Kensington and Chelsea Foundation commissioned a report, 'Poverty and Prosperity in Kensington and Chelsea: Understanding Inequalities in a Borough of Extremes'. It was similar to mine, though far more extensive and professionally produced, as it had been funded.

The K&C Foundation report focused on middle super-output areas rather than lower super-output areas, which I had used (and which are more finely detailed). Nonetheless, its findings confirmed many of my earlier concerns. Having these confirmed by a charity and a professional external research organisation was encouragingly vindicating – though the findings were, of course, depressing.

In relation to education, while I was very aware of disparities, 'Poverty and Prosperity in Kensington and Chelsea' had some surprises for me. It stated that K&C has the highest rate of school exclusion in London, the highest rate of permanent exclusion in London, and the highest rate of managed moves (where families are persuaded to move the student voluntarily to a Pupil Referral Unit (PRU) or exclusion school, without having a negative comment added to their school record).

They also found that the proportion of BAME (Black, Asian and minority ethnic) students who were excluded was four times greater than the proportion in the rest of England, and that the performance gap for BAME students was four times worse than the England average, with education inequalities across the board almost double the London average.

Just over a quarter (28%) of all state school children were eligible for free school meals. Continuing the issues relating to the effect of poor housing on educational outcomes, in North Kensington the report found an average of 20% overcrowding among school students, and the second highest number of households in temporary accommodation in England.

Unsurprisingly, there was still a lot of pressure on mental health services for all ages, post-Grenfell, but disappointingly the local services were rated in the worst 20% in England. This was all terrible news, but I did feel vindicated. I approached the Council to see how they intended to respond to this devastating official report. Their response was: 'The report was to inform themselves how best to allocate funding.'

So the Council seemed to be perfectly happy to maintain the status quo, where they fail people and local charities fill in the gaps.

Even though the Council set up an Inequality Working Group in early 2021 after my second report came out (not as a consequence of it, of course!), many people feared that this was tokenistic political posturing. A colleague and I dutifully sat in meetings where fine words and targets were bandied about, and then a 'final report' was to be written. We had carried out zero actual work. We both resigned from the Working Group. Once again, there had been lots of 'activity', but no change.

We are led to believe that the Council has changed since the days when it spent £24.4 million on paving Exhibition Road to welcome visitors to the London Olympics, while monetising parks and play spaces and cutting free swimming so that low-income families would find it harder to enjoy sports. But is this true? This is, after all, the Council that closed the last council-run residential care home in the borough in 2014 and finally sold the site in 2017 for £75 million, moving residents far out of the borough. In 2018 it was judged by the Care Quality Commission (CQC) to be the fourth worst provider of social care in the country. How it has changed!

During the first Covid lockdown, many of the food banks run by churches and voluntary groups hoped to get funding from the Council. Some did. This, however, came with strings attached – the monitoring of recipients. The various food banks, food pantries (where a small sum is charged to buy supplies), and hot food suppliers (who often bring food directly to homes), have differing eligibility standards. Some need a reference, from a GP, Citizen's Advice or other referral agent. Others simply give food to those who ask for it; this can be to people who live 'off-line', are undocumented, are street homeless, or have poor communication skills. When challenged on this infringement of recipients' privacy (which caused embarrassment or humiliation) the then Director of Communities responded: 'This is to ascertain who actually needs the food, and who just wants it.'

Which displays, so eloquently, the total poverty of spirit that was sadly still prevalent at RBKC Council.

Chapter 3

THE SULTAN AND MRS BRAITHWAITE

Inequalities in the Royal Borough are not focused solely on income and health inequity. A system of obvious and hidden subsidies favours those with more money than the 17,000 households living in social housing, the 29,000 living in private rented flats, and of course the 2,000 households in temporary accommodation.

One of these hidden subsidies is the way in which council tax is charged. In the run-up to the 2015 general election, there was a row in the Labour Party about council tax and the Labour leader Ed Miliband's proposal for a mansion tax, which would be worked out depending on the current value of a home, supposedly making payments fairer. The Labour Group of Councillors, of which I was leader at the time, did not support this, and went public with our campaign of dissent. It made no sense for someone who had bought a house in the 1970s in a 'bad' area and refurbished it and brought up their family there to be punished with an extra tax because their long-term family home had shot up in value and was now worth over £1 million.

Some residents I talked to at the time were terrified of the mansion tax proposal. One of my neighbours was reduced to tears by it. It may not have been intended to include long-time freeholders, but it was poorly drafted and poorly presented; the right-wing media had a field day. There are 12,400 homes in Band H for council tax in the borough, meaning they are worth over £2 million; 7,000 of these have been owned by the same people since 1999. Some of these owners may indeed be asset-rich and cash-poor – how many are lived in by the original purchasers and how many are owned by Grosvenors or Cadogans and let out is not currently known. But I know of several Black families who bought houses in North Kensington in the 1960s and 1970s because no one would rent to them. Many still live in these homes, with two or three generations living together.

My 2014 research on inequalities in relation to the percentage of household income that went on council tax unearthed a bizarre fact: the Sultan of Brunei, reportedly worth $30 billion, was paying just £10 a week more in council tax for his 16-bedroom mansion in Kensington Palace Gardens than a retired African-Caribbean woman was paying for a three-bedroomed council flat in North Kensington. Bloomberg News ran the story, 'The Sultan and Mrs Braithwaite', to wide media interest.

How did we get into this situation?

The current council tax system is based on 1991 house prices. RBKC has one of the lowest council tax rates in the country: effectively yet another subsidy to freeholders. Interestingly, the RBKC annual resident survey found year after year that residents would rather pay a little more council tax than lose any Council-provided services – a preference that the Council chose to ignore year after year. Residents wanted council tax to be raised to cover rising adult social care costs and provide support for people with special needs. Indeed, when it was eventually increased to cover rising adult social care costs in 2020, few people complained.

Other subsidies for homeowners in 2014 included:

- capital gains tax relief, which in 2015 cost the country £6 billion a year
- no property tax, which cost £11 billion a year
- the Right to Buy subsidy, which cost £2 billion a year at the time
- shared ownership subsidies
- help for buy-to-let landlords, with interest-only mortgages.

Since then, there have been numerous other incentives to encourage people to buy, such as starter homes. This scheme gave first-time buyers a 20% discount on a new home (another subsidy to developers); however, the government had to admit in 2019 that not a single home had been bought this way.

In many countries, for example Spain, the freeholder or lease-holder pays council tax, not the tenant. It is a strange system indeed that punishes tenants and leaves owners – whose assets are increasing in value while bringing in revenue – unscathed. But in the UK all the income tax breaks and profits are in the hands of the freeholder or leaseholder, while tenants are disadvantaged or even punished in countless ways. It is just one example of the widespread and deliberate 'trickle up' of assets, subsidies, money and power. Here's another. In 2004, before I joined the Council, the RBKC Cabinet had agreed a 'development framework' for some properties in Elm

Park Gardens. I knew the street well, as it was on the way to my primary school in Old Brompton Road from my home off King's Road. I must have been down that street, from childhood to adulthood, thousands of times. We had friends who lived there in those days, and I have friends who live there now.

Elm Park Gardens was in a very poor state of repair after the war. In 1949 the Council had taken it over and it had been used for social housing since then. It had, like many streets of Chelsea mansion blocks, become quite grand over the years, with numerous very lucky leaseholders living there, along with some famous residents and titled, classic K&C 'genteel poor'. The Council caretakers were called porters. Some residents thought they were a cut above most Council estates, as indeed they were. Soon after I joined the Council I became aware that planning permission had been granted to convert some thirty-six empty basements in Elm Park Gardens into homes – twenty-three for the open market and thirteen 'affordable'. The permission surprised me, as the permission application stated that these basement units were considered 'air space' or 'storage'. I knew that some had been lived in, and the rest, although they were derelict, were certainly capable of being refurbished and turned into very nice flats. Given how many potential social rented homes there were in the basements of 1–110 Elm Park Gardens, I felt uneasy about the idea of converting most of them into market properties.

In 2008 I joined the Kensington and Chelsea Tenant Management Organisation (KCTMO) as a Board member. KCTMO was an 'arms-length' tenant's management organisation, with a tenant-led Board, that manages the entire portfolio of 9,000 Council residential properties. Encouraged by an Elm Park Gardens tenant, I decided to investigate further. I visited the area several times, counted the empty basements, and explored several of them. They were huge, with high ceilings and large windows, many with direct access to the communal gardens. Some had original Victorian fitted kitchen shelving and cupboards, butlers' pantries and sinks, and massive cast-iron ranges. They were quite beautiful. Between 70 and 110 potential basement homes had been empty for over fifty years. It was shocking, really.

In spring 2009 I met the RBKC Director of Property, who explained patiently that because these basements were 'air space, and not registered for council tax . . . they would be kept out of the Housing Revenue Account'. In other words, profits from selling them as derelict shell units would go to the General Fund, to be spent on whatever the Council chose. At the time Council reserves were £204 million. Soon after my inquiry, in 2011 the Cabinet decided to defer sales of most of the shell units, as the global financial crash had affected the property market and they wanted to wait for the flats' value to increase. They put three out of eighteen for sale, to 'test the market'. In other words, they kept property off the market to contribute to a shortage, and thereby raise prices.

The RBKC Core Strategy at the time had a housing target of building a total of 600 additional units a year, of which at least 200 should be affordable (including social rent), the remainder for market sale or rent: converting the basements would have been a big step to meeting its annual target. But when I brought up the issue of Elm Park Gardens at a Housing Committee meeting, the Cabinet Member for Housing objected to my request for the basements to be converted into housing, saying: 'But people need somewhere to store their grand pianos.' A bizarre response from a Councillor living in a parallel universe.

I sought advice from the Empty Homes Agency, who suggested that I write to the Secretary of State to ask that a 'Public Request Ordering Disposal' (PROD) be sent to the Council requiring them to either refurbish and use the properties, or sell them. We agreed it was a case of poor asset management. At the time, 6,000 households were on the Council waiting list. Those 110 properties had to be mobilised, one way or the other. I sent my request to the Secretary of State in September 2009 and had an acknowledgement by return of post and a full response in November 2009, after the Council had been contacted.

The Council did what it always does when challenged on such matters – deny it, then fix it. They denied there was any issue with the basements, and stated they had a 'firm intention to develop the basement flats into mixed tenured residential units'. They then brought their plans forward. By spring 2010 they were 'progressing' with their plans, which were for a mix of social rented and key-worker homes. By this time they were all considered to be within the Housing Revenue Account (magically no longer the General Fund). They continued with their plan to sell off shell units for private development, making a gross profit of £13 million, with a net profit after 'enabling works' to improve infrastructure by updating gas and electrical works, of £8 million. The project was claimed by RBKC in 2010 as a 'source of real pride to us at the Royal Borough'.

In May 2012, a Cabinet report stated that capital receipts from the sale of shell units at Elm Park Gardens would be used to build new homes and refurbish existing homes. Some of this went to a 'Hidden Homes' project of infill on two estates, and the remainder – clearly not enough – went towards the cost of refurbishing

Grenfell Tower, whose original windows leaked, heating and hot water failed regularly, and the lifts were often out of order. In 2012, after a consultation with residents in Lancaster West, the KCTMO stated that their proposals for improvements to Grenfell Tower had 'overwhelming support'. At the time, they did. But that support didn't last long.

I found another unaccountable example of empty homes much nearer to my home. In 2009 I noticed that a large corner building two doors down from my home had been empty for a while. When I moved into North Ken in 1986 it was a care home, then a children's home for Somali war refugees. I well remember the scared, wide-eyed children arriving in winter and local people donating warm clothes to them. We watched them grow and saw them play football in the street. They lived there for many years. Many eventually found jobs locally and stayed in the area. The building was then used as a hostel for homeless young adults. We got to know them and they also became part of the local picture, but eventually the hostel closed and the building stood empty.

I discovered that it was owned by the Council and had been let to Octavia Housing. It was squatted for a while: when the squatters were evicted, the Council put security guards in to protect it. The Council then explained at a committee meeting that it would have to sell the building as it had been damaged by the squatters, who had taken out plumbing and wiring. So I visited one day. It wasn't true. The building was scruffy but functional, its plumbing and wiring intact.

In April 2010 the Cabinet Member for Housing said we could no longer provide additional social rented housing in the borough because buying new freehold land was too expensive. This ignored the fact that the Council owned numerous plots of land at the time, and ignored this building, Adelaide House, which had sixteen bedrooms. An almost identical building across the road which was owned by a housing association had been converted to eleven social rented homes. But the Council would not listen.

There was quite a row about the lawful use of the building, as its designation of C2 ('a residential institution') meant it came under the category of 'social and community use' (or CK1). In theory, if it could not be reused as a residential institution or for a different social and community use, its designation would fail and it could be sold, with the funds being ring-fenced for other social and community use in the borough. Needless to say, all the Council's research found that it could not be reused for any CK1 use.

A local prep school attempted to buy the property, to convert it and put 200 children in there to increase private education capacity. After a huge local campaign – which, interestingly, was supported by some of the Somalis who had lived there – it was refused planning permission and the sale did not go through. In the end this valuable property was left empty for eleven years, with the Council wasting taxpayers' money on security the whole time. Inevitably, it finally went on the market and a developer bought it to convert it into private luxury residential homes. The Leader of the Council was comfortable with this change of use: 'Wealthy people from all over the world want to own property in Kensington and Chelsea, and that's no bad thing. It's good for our shops, good for our restaurants, good for employment, and it's good for the Exchequer too.'

The flats were completed in summer 2021 after being empty for eleven years. When I asked in 2016 where the funds from the sale of the property were to be spent I was told by the Town Clerk, 'Surely all Council activities are "social and community use".' Hardly.

When I was first elected to the Council in 2006, I imagined that a large part of my role would be helping residents who could not access support due to barriers such as physical or mental ill-health, language or literacy barriers. I never imagined that KCTMO and the housing associations would be so badly managed that I'd spend days – or even weeks – chasing them for even an acknowledgement of an email. In an attempt to improve the housing providers response to casework inquiries, in 2009 I wrote a report, 'Room for Improvement: The handling of casework by registered social landlords'. I sent it out, using anonymised real-life cases, to all our social landlords. I hoped it would shame them into action.

One case involved a family with adult children sharing one bedroom, so the parent had to sleep on the sofa. Noisy neighbours, who played loud music at night, made the parent's life a misery. Eventually the parent had a heart attack and was hospitalised. After five years of misery, the parent passed away.

Another case involved a couple, one of whom had a debilitating illness. A drug den next door made their difficult lives unbearable, and even after I had emailed the housing association thirty-eight times with no response, there was no solution. The couple were so desperate, they considered double suicide. They were finally rehoused after all their neighbours sent letters of appeal.

I often left phone messages for KCTMO that were never answered. One case involved me sending sixty-five emails. Eight were responded to, but resulted in no solution (to a case involving a disabled family member living in unsuitable accommodation). Some

TMO officers were very rude and even bullying – I witnessed this personally. There were ever more disgraceful cases. While details in my 'Room for Improvement' report were anonymised, I added accurate details when I sent it to the chief executives of the housing providers, KCTMO and housing associations.

The Council and housing associations refuted all my findings and objected strongly to the evidence I had sent them about un-answered emails and the rudeness of officers. 'Deny it, then fix it' was their attitude. But for a while, at least, I found that responses were a little better.

Sitting on the Housing Committee in 2009, I delved for the first time into the SHMA: the Strategic Housing Market Assessment. This is an annual report written by the Council Planning team which reviews the current state of affairs and sets targets for housing with reference to national, London-wide and local plan-ning policy. Among its findings in 2009 were the following: the average household in K&C comprised two people, but nearly 50% were single-person households; 44% of homes were owner-occu-pied, with the rest split evenly into social rented and private rented. It reported 3,037 'vacant' homes – that is, not second homes. The mean gross household income, which included unemployed people, was reported to be £11,000, while the median was £52,000. Under a third (30%) of households earned less than £20,000, while 30% earned over £100,000. Just over 4,000 homes were deemed to be Category 1 hazards – the worst possible – in relation to poor heating and ill health. As we observed anecdotally, people who work in the borough cannot afford to live in the borough. Overcrowding, at 5.5%, was double the national average, while under-occupation was 16.4%. There was a net surplus of private rented properties, but the overwhelming need was for social rented and intermediate (partially subsidised) rented homes. While some of these figures are different, this is due to varying methods of calculation that use contrary indicators.

In summary, according to the SHMA of 2009, the need for accommodation over the next twenty years was:

> Market homes +1,924
> Intermediate homes +451
> Social rented homes +4,315

Meanwhile, Council-owned properties lay empty. Aside from the pitiful rate of turnaround time (over three months) between tenants for social housing, there were long-term properties that the Council seemed to have forgotten about. We were finally provided with a list of these properties: some were school-keeper houses, some park lodges, and some were flats formerly used by caretakers. All of them were in the General Fund, not the Housing Revenue Account (HRA), and had previously been used as accommodation for workers who needed to live in the borough and preferably on-site. We estimated there were around fifty. Over time, some were used by squatters, which was legal at the time. We expected that, once these properties had been 'reclaimed' by the Council through eviction, they would be brought back into use for families on the waiting list. But no. Instead the Council installed security guards in these properties to keep them empty. Many of us thought this was verging on criminality. Over the years, rather than reconsider the use of these potential social homes, they were sold off or developed. Two sites were used for social need, one redeveloped as a children's home, and a park lodge – after being kept empty for over twelve years by security guards – was finally (in summer 2021) about to be demolished for development as social housing. Homeless families could have lived there in the years these homes were kept empty by security guards.

Without Sadiq Khan the Mayor of London's 2020 funding commitment of £30 million to RBKC to build homes for social rent, this inexcusably long-term empty park-keeper's house could also have been sold into the private market. The funds meant the Council eventually used the site to develop affordable homes. Why was this detached home with a large garden kept empty for twelve years?

In September 2010, as the proposed cuts to housing benefit, local housing allowance and temporary accommodation subsidy were approaching, the RBKC Housing team wrote a devastating report for the Housing Committee. It concluded: 'The potential for central London and the Royal Borough to effectively become a residential no-go area for anybody on a low income looking to rent is real . . . [including] long-standing families who may have lived in the borough all of their lives.'

The Royal Borough of Kensington and Chelsea – a no-go area for the poor, as concluded by a housing officer. It hit the front page of the local papers.

In response, the then Cabinet Member for Housing said: 'People will have to move to find alternative homes that they can afford.' For a Cabinet made up of millionaires, with second (or indeed first) homes elsewhere, moving home must seem like a minor inconvenience. They have zero understanding of low-income families who depend on their local network for their well-being;

of the devastation that would be caused if they were forced to move away.

In late 2012, there were rumours that the Leader of the Council and the Chief Executive of RBKC had been in discussion with the Leader of Peterborough City Council with a view to spending £50 million to buy land in Peterborough to be developed as social housing to move 'ambitious young families' off the waiting list: one hundred miles from London. At first the Council denied that it was anything more than a cautious chat, but details were then leaked that the Council was considering this as a very serious possibility. A Freedom of Information (FoI) request eventually revealed that the proposal went as far as getting indicative build costs, along with costs of providing shared ownership homes and social housing. Discussions continued into 2013, according to the FoI, that 'revolved around mutual benefits of a collaboration between each authority other than housing'. The FoI response continued: 'These benefits included cultural exchanges between schools, sharing the tri-borough safeguarding work . . . sharing Peterborough CC environmental work and potential energy benefits, and finally liturgical, festival and museum links.'

What all this comprised was not revealed in detail. A copy of a full draft proposal tabled in November 2013 was never shared. In any event, the proposal to socially cleanse 'ambitious young families' from the borough, at a cost of £50 million, went precisely nowhere.

In 2014/15, to get a broader picture of these problems, I conducted research on housing inequalities in the borough, with our then parliamentary candidate. I wrote a report on various aspects of housing in Kensington, 'Housing in Kensington; where will your children live?', April 2015. Across the borough in 2015 there were 89,000 residential properties, of which 25,000 had no electors registered. According to the 2011 Census, one in fifty homes was empty and one in ten was either empty or a second home. In wards such as Golborne almost none were empty, whereas in Queen's Gate ward, just south of Kensington Palace, one in five was empty or a second home. In total there were 3,031 empty homes registered by the Empty Homes Agency, of which just under a half, 1,215 were long-term empty.

Over 9,000 households were on the waiting list for Council properties at the time. Knowing how bad this looked, the Council simply removed from the waiting list anyone who was not in 'priority need', reducing the list to around 2,000 households. This left 7,000 overcrowded or homeless households who had no hope of being housed by their Council, ever.

According to the Census, there were 9,303 second homes in Kensington and Chelsea; 11,733 residents of K&C had a second home elsewhere in the UK, and 17,974 residents had a second home outside the UK. In December 2019, before the pandemic changed the profile of short-term lettings, 5,274 homes in the borough were registered for Airbnb, the fourth highest number in London, and the most expensive borough in which to rent an Airbnb.

There may be some double-counting involved; nonetheless, that's potentially 43,000 – almost half the borough's homes – that are not lived in permanently, if at all, and 9,000 households waiting for housing.

According to Transparency UK, 7.3% of properties (that's 5,838 homes in the borough) were at the time owned by companies registered in an offshore secrecy jurisdiction or tax haven; some of these are included in the figures above. So if we were able to take legal action against empty homes – and currently we aren't, though there are moves to this end – some of the owners would be almost impossible to track down.

And this problem is only getting worse. In the seven months from December 2013 to July 2014, K&C lost 220 homes net. This was due to a combination of de-conversions (large houses sub-divided into flats being converted back into single homes), amalgamations and demolitions versus new homes built. Meanwhile, 63% of children in Golborne ward lived in overcrowded homes. In 2012 there were 800 'housing gains', which is what homes given planning permission are called, but only 100 were actually built. Some of these were deliberately held back for as long as possible by developers to increase their price. While this practice clearly disadvantages a council supposedly wishing to improve its delivery of new homes, RBKC Council was involved in this practice itself. A Council-owned site in Lots Road, Cremorne Wharf, was at the point of having to hand over a lease to the Thames Tideway Tunnel project for several years. The Council brought forward a planning application for part of the site to build homes, being frank about doing this to increase the value of the site. In the end, for reasons that were not made public, the application was withdrawn. But this was not the first or the last time when the Council was clearly complicit in pushing up the value of its own property assets while bemoaning the high cost of property – and the necessity of unfortunately having to move low-income residents out of the borough, as we shall see.

In 2014, at the time of my first report on inequalities, the average home in K&C cost £1.2 million. To afford a mortgage on this home you would need to earn £250,000 pa. To buy a shared ownership home in North Kensington, you would need to earn £45,000 pa for a one-bedroom flat or £60,000 for a two-bedroom flat. This led to situations like the one where residents of Catalyst Housing's soon-to-be-bulldozed Wornington Green were repeatedly told in 2010 that they would be able to buy a shared ownership flat after their estate had been developed. The reality, of course, was that not a single one could afford it.

Local housing allowance was set up to support families living in expensive private rented accommodation. Heavy cuts to it were made by the incoming Tory/Lib Dem coalition government in 2010, resulting in up to 2,000 families being squeezed out of the borough, some into temporary accommodation, two-thirds of which was outside the borough. The Council received a fixed amount of funding from the government per family in temporary accommodation, based on local market rates; if they could source homes more cheaply, they kept the 'surplus'. In 2012 this 'surplus' – or profit – was £1.12 million. This clearly gave the Council an incentive to place families in temporary accommodation a long way out of the borough, where rents are cheaper, then bank the remainder.

The bedroom tax, set up to incentivise older people whose families had moved out to downsize their homes, affected 1,000 Council households in K&C. Interim support was given to people in this situation, in the form of a discretionary housing payment, but this was for a set period only. The KCTMO made a great fuss about a scheme of 'enhanced refurbishments' of smaller homes to encourage under-occupying households to move. The reality was, there were very few suitable smaller homes available, and the 'enhanced' level of refurbishment was, frankly, what every empty flat should have received to provide a decent home. They called this enhanced refurbishment 'Kensington Standard'. Remember the name.

Meanwhile, for those waiting to be housed, whom the Council had a duty to house, the option was temporary accommodation (TA) – though 'temporary' was not really the best word, since some households had been waiting for years. The longest period I've heard of for a family in TA was thirteen years. In 2010 1,117 households in the borough were in TA: a total of 2,942 individuals. Of them, 1,300 were under eighteen.

One contributor to the one-third of TA within the borough was the Housing Association Letting Scheme (HALS). This relates to previously Council-owned homes that had been bought under Right to Buy. They had subsequently been let to housing associations, which then sublet them to the Council for TA, so they could charge the full market rate – and then be recompensed by the government. So a Council flat let to a tenant paying £120/week could have as a neighbour a Right to Buy flat, let to a housing association then re-let to the Council at full market rate for temporary accommodation, which cost up to £350/week, for which tenants had to apply to the government for housing benefit. This must be one of the most twisted examples ever of misuse of government subsidies.

People living in Right to Buy homes in the borough are, in some senses, the lucky ones: as I said earlier, two-thirds of families in TA are moved out of the borough. Over the years the Council, rather than renting homes from private landlords, has begun to buy homes outside the borough for this purpose. Whether this is simply a sensible and economic way of keeping people housed, or yet another profit-making scheme, is hard to say. But between 2015 and 2021 the Council spent £20 million on purchasing homes for TA outside the borough, and had plans to spend a further £40 million over the following three years. That makes £60 million on keeping families housed outside the borough, while the Council tells us that the small number of new homes for social rent that the Council is developing itself, using funds donated by the Mayor of London, must be cross-subsidised by private homes. Why not keep the funds to be spent in the borough? I have yet to receive a coherent answer to this.

All these cuts and changes to eligibility for social housing caused genuine hardship, and our Councillors' surgeries began to fill with tenants who had been devastated by the potential loss of their homes, or with homeless or overcrowded families desperately needing to be rehoused.

Labour Councillors have always been told that there is nowhere in the borough to build social housing. This simply isn't true. There were then, and there still are, plots of land of various sizes across the borough. But when the Council decides to build on them, they build private homes 'to bring in much-needed revenue': this is nonsense from a Council with such extraordinary levels of reserves – reserves boosted by revenue underspends. The land the Council has claimed not to own included plots that were later developed for private housing, including Young Street car park, Cremorne Wharf, Edenham Residential Care Home, Hortensia Road, Middle Row School playground, Marlborough School playground, Holland Park School southern playground, and no doubt numerous street properties of various sizes, such as

Adelaide House near me, which was sold off on the quiet with 'capital receipts' hidden away in the Council's annual Statements of Accounts.

In 2015 there were 6,890 Council homes, plus 1,890 leasehold. A further 17,600 homes were let by housing associations. These numbers were regularly eroded by 'disposals': when a property became vacant, it could be sold on the open market. Alternatively, due to another filthy piece of coalition legislation, when a tenant moved out, in some circumstances the home could be re-let at an 'affordable' rent – which in RBKC was 60% of the market rent – though in some cases housing associations charge up to 80% of market rent, which is not 'affordable' in any sense of the word to social tenants on modest incomes, particularly in Kensington and Chelsea. Around fifty social rented properties a year were lost to the private market at the time; these 'disposals' are hard to track and housing associations do not like to share this information, but we knew that the stock of social housing kept dwindling.

When I became MP, my casework expanded hugely, and much of it was related to housing. We tackled 11,000 cases, including around 500 Grenfell-related cases, which of course all came at once immediately after my election, and each meant dealing with traumatised people with specific needs. With so many people coming to me for help, it was easier to see housing trends in the area. Nearly half of the cases my team and I dealt with were related to housing. In November 2017 I published a report, 'After Grenfell – Housing and Inequality in Kensington and Chelsea: "The most unequal borough in Britain"'. The Council didn't like it one bit. I was trolled on social media as a way to distract from the damaging report I had published. But the report, and I, prevailed.

In 2018 we did a casework round-up. It found that: in Kensington the average house price was £1,404,250, which was 610% higher than the national average wage, while wages were only 110% higher than the national average, putting home ownership out of reach for most residents. We found that the Council was failing in its duty to give advice to homeless people and then failing in its duty to house those they had a duty to house, instead putting them in long-term temporary accommodation, often far from their school, work, further education and social networks. We also found that the Council and housing associations did not invest enough to maintain their properties but let them fall into disrepair, ignoring requests from tenants to tackle repairs. This was not simply because of a lack of resources: social landlords ignored tenants' concerns and treated them with disdain, while the complex maze of contractors and subcontractors supposedly managing properties created silo working and removed accountability and transparency. In 2017, RBKC was approached by 1,159 homeless households. The Council agreed to help 674. Of these, 263 were placed in B&B accommodation (with shared bathrooms, kitchens and other facilities). Some of these homeless households were offered places as far away as Welwyn Garden City, Dartford, Croydon, Bedfordshire, High Wycombe, Medway and Havering – all huge distances from the borough. These were allocated by direct offer, which is a one-time-only offer – if it is refused, the household is taken off the waiting list. One very vulnerable constituent was offered a house in a coastal town and had to accept it. They lost their job and all their personal contacts and support, and fell into depression and illness.

We found that many homeless households asking for help were subjected to 'gatekeeping': they were discouraged from applying for help at their first contact with the Council, so they did not proceed with the application. They were not informed of their rights and therefore were not formally informed that they are not eligible for help.

In 2017/18, 2,235 households were living in temporary accommodation, the highest on record. This figure excluded those made homeless by the Grenfell Tower fire, who were housed under a separate system. Of those in TA, 227 were in B&Bs, 143 in hostels and 1,836 in the private sector. A Freedom of Information request found that 346 households were placed in unsuitable TA: this could be due to the property being overcrowded, unaffordable, not suitable for medical reasons, or where they were under threat of violence (e.g. a hostel).

The government's rules for placing people in B&B accommodation is clear. Households with children or pregnant women should not be in a B&B for longer than six weeks: 'Wherever possible, housing authorities should avoid using B&B accommodation as accommodation for homeless applicants' and B&Bs should always be 'used for the shortest time possible'. However, the Freedom of Information request revealed that the RBKC had a habit of placing households in B&Bs, and many were stuck there for years. Between 2014 and 2018 the Council placed over 1,000 households in B&Bs, including numerous children.

As we have seen, the Council has been buying homes to use as temporary accommodation outside the borough for some time. Between 2015 and 2020 it spent a further £12 million on this programme. The 2021/22 Council Budget planned to spend a further £18 million over the following three years, but there was an additional budget line proposing to spend a further £40 million on buying TA over three years. So it seems the Council cannot afford to buy or otherwise provide homes in RBKC (the 'we have nowhere to build' fallacy) but are prepared to spend £60 million on moving homeless residents out of the borough into so-called temporary accommodation, which can last for up to 13 years: in other words 'permanent temporary'. Whether this is better or worse than the 2013 proposal to spend £50 million to transport homeless households to Peterborough is open to question. Either way, this is still happening, and the Council is continuing to make what officers claim are 'modest profits' from it.

Housing associations often come under fire for their poor care of tenants, lack of cyclical maintenance, lack of response regarding repairs, missing appointments where tenants have had to take time off work, and general rude or dismissive staff. One housing officer actually told a tenant not to contact me as MP, telling them: 'Drop the MP, and I'll help you.' The tenant said they were treated 'like a criminal'. This is shocking and indefensible, but not unusual. In 2019 I published a further report on housing casework. I called it 'Drop the MP'. The officer who made that comment was reported to his superiors – but kept his job.

One way of providing new 'affordable' homes (costing less than market price, not necessarily social rent level) is via S106 payments: this means that developers of large private developments must pay a percentage of their profits towards social housing or, preferably, build it on-site. This rarely happens. The target for total new homes in RBKC, set by the London Plan in 2012, was 733 per year. Around one-third should be for affordable or social rent, so about 270 per year. The Annual Monitoring Report shows the number of affordable homes built. This was the record over ten years:

2010/11:   61
2011/12:   23
2012/13:   4
2013/14:   46
2014/15:   196
2015/16:   67
2016/17:   23 + 68 (Housing Association homes transferred
            to RBKC, post-Grenfell, so not really a gain)
2017/18:   42 (all private to affordable, post-Grenfell)
2018/19:   0
2019/20:   0

Due to the 'difficulties' involved for RBKC in delivering homes, the Council has managed to negotiate a lower number (448 per year) from 2021. In 2020/21 some of the S106 funding of £14 million was set aside to support the Mayoral contribution to build social housing.

In 2014/15 the net number of homes lost included those lost to demolitions. In 2021 it did not. In 2017 151 homes were lost at Grenfell Tower and Grenfell Walk, but they have not been accounted for. Catalyst Housing's development at Wornington Green is the first post-war estate to be developed in the borough. Every single one of the 541 homes there is due to be demolished in phases and replaced with double the number of private homes. But the Council don't subtract losses through demolition. However, they do count the replacement social rented flats as 'net additional', which they clearly are not.

In 2010 we were told that Wornington Green was 'short of 201 bedrooms' and that development was essential to house overcrowded families; the estate had been given planning permission on that basis. However, we heard that 'maybe fifteen to twenty extra homes' would be built, so the guarantee that families could return after development was, in essence, untrue.

So where are our Wornington families now? In 2021, with the demolition and rebuilding halfway through, many families have disappeared, some have returned, Grenfell homeless have found homes there, and some are still living in their old homes, surrounded by the daily crash and drill and dust of a construction site.

As well as the preceding issues, there are continued failures on behalf of the Council, social landlords and private landlords to properly maintain the properties for which they are responsible. Some landlords are worse than others. The Council is 'less bad' as housing manager than KCTMO was at maintenance; nonetheless, the standard of maintenance is often appalling. Damp, black mould, leaks, collapsed ceilings, rotten floors and rodent infestations make tenants' lives miserable. This goes alongside poor enforcement of rules and regulations relating to antisocial behaviour and harassment. Some believe this neglect is deliberate, to force tenants to move out of the area into cheaper, possibly newer and better maintained accommodation. I put it down to incompetence and lack of care.

Many residents imagine that the Council sells off residential properties for profit. Over the years the Council's Statements of Accounts show regular 'disposals', often adding up to millions of pounds. Some of them are land or 'other assets'. These would include the various playgrounds and car parks that have been developed – and of course the former Thamesbrook Care Home off King's Road, which netted £75 million. The profits from all of these went to the General Fund: the funds are kept by the Council and go straight into capital reserves, and the Council is free to use them for whatever it wishes.

Homes in the Housing Revenue Account, however, are dealt with very differently. Three-quarters of the income from 'disposals of dwellings' goes to the government, and the remainder must be spent on new Council homes or the refurbishment of existing homes – such as at Grenfell Tower. So why on earth would the Council continue to sell off dwellings in the HRA when all they recoup is a paltry million or half-million here and there? They have sold off entire houses in Billing Street and in St Luke's Street, both in Chelsea, which would have made decent homes for some of our larger, or multi-generational, homeless families. You have to wonder: if it isn't done for the money, is this simply ideological? Could it be that the Council doesn't want social tenants living in 'nice' areas?

What we have seen in this chapter is the Council fudging housing statistics; finding new ways of counting available homes; gatekeeping homeless household applications; preparing to spend £50 million to move homeless households to Peterborough; proposing to spend £60 million on 'permanent temporary' housing from which it would make a 'modest profit' on income – and of course profit from the asset. The Council may report that there is 'nowhere to build social housing', but it was prepared to magically find space to build private housing on every car park and school playground, for sale or rent. Is the Council really focused on attracting wealthy incomers while transporting low-income families out of the borough?

The next chapter focuses on the Council's brutal and wide-reaching programme to redevelop Council estates. RBKC's plan to be a 'no-go area for the poor' was gathering pace.

Chapter 4

FIGHTING GENTRIFICATION,
ONE CUPCAKE AT A TIME

Kensington and Chelsea is a beautiful part of London, with lovely parks (in some areas); very good schools (if you can get your children into them); wonderful galleries and museums (mostly still free, which is a life-saver for parents, as I know only too well); and great shopping and tree-lined streets (in the wealthier areas, anyway). A lot of people would love to live in such a lively and culturally rich area. The problem is that there is not an infinite availability of homes for incomers.

What many local authorities see as 'regeneration' is simply a euphemism for driving up the value of housing, bringing in new people on middle to high incomes, and squeezing out local people on a low income. It is profit-driven, not people-driven, and it forces up the costs of housing for everyone. When senior RBKC Tory Councillors bleated that the cost of housing was driving their own children out of the borough, we tried not to show our exasperation. For years RBKC Council has been 100% complicit in driving up the cost of housing. And for some it has been a class war too, to drive out what some see as the 'undeserving poor' low-income households.

The Georgian square where I was born was clearly built for the gentry, but war and a damaged economy brought down house prices, allowing middle-earning families like mine to settle there. Our immediate neighbours were a dentist and a vicar. Much of the square was scruffy and family-friendly, and very mixed ethnically, including a lot of European refugees. Over the years it has reverted to its intended inhabitants, with many homes refurbished to a very high standard; I doubt that NHS hospital doctors, dentists and vicars could afford to live there now.

Since 1986 I have lived in a flat in a Victorian terraced house in North Ken. It was built in 1892 for the wealthy middle classes, with servants' quarters and a mews behind for horses and carriages. I did some research: my house was never actually lived in as a family home. It lay empty and unsold for five years then was bought by two sisters to run as a lodging house. That was the fate of many houses in the Ladbroke Grove area, which was hastily developed when the Metropolitan line reached it. Many houses here were taken over in the 1950s and 1960s, after years of near dereliction, by housing associations. When I moved into North Ken the area was still run-down and most of the houses had been converted, cheaply, into flats.

Gentrification is another matter entirely from these kinds of fluctuations in housing. North Ken houses like mine may attract wealthier people now than they did thirty years ago, but true gentrification takes place when a working-class area, like most of Golborne ward, is 'discovered' and infiltrated by high-end coffee shops and impossibly expensive designer shops that cater for a (sometimes imagined) wealthier group of incomers, not for local people. This is gentrification. Over the years many businesses have moved in, imagining that Golborne Road will be a goldmine, but have lost a lot of money. It's a lovely road, and the Council has spent a fortune making it lovelier, but it's in a very, very poor area. There is zero trickle-down from these incoming businesses: in fact, the area has got poorer in the last ten years.

We had a long-standing debate within the Council and local communities, and urban design academics I was in contact with, on gentrification vs regeneration vs social cleansing in the mid-2010s. Eventually, I came up with a definition:

Regeneration is an aim, not a process. Development or redevelopment carried out with intelligence, good planning and modest expectations of profit **can** result in regeneration. 'Regeneration' comprises an uplift of economic and social benefits and well-being for existing residents and businesses over the long term. Means other than development – such as refurbishment – can also achieve regeneration in its true sense.

If development only achieves improvements in visual amenity, built form, additional residential or business units, but does not produce other long-term sustainable economic or social benefits for the existing population, it is not regeneration.

Other outcomes – intended or unintended – such as displacement of long-term residents and local businesses and services is not regeneration. This is social cleansing, pure and simple.

In this chapter we will see how RBKC Council, after the change of government in 2010, became rampantly developer-friendly, focusing its energies on inflating land and property prices while supporting a process of managed decline of much of our social housing to soften up residents for more drastic change. This process was enthusiastically embraced by the then Deputy Leader, who was a 'man of his time' in the worst possible sense. As the Leader of the Council announced at a property conference, 'Kensington and Chelsea is open for business'.

Around this time Stella McCartney 'discovered' Golborne Road and set up her design studio there. Her presence was heavily referenced in hyperbolic estate agent literature. Prices rocketed, for homes and for businesses. A local friend who was herself a designer told me, 'Stella McCartney drove me out', after the rent on her shop doubled. Meanwhile, the wealthy newcomers complained that visiting taxis had nowhere to stop due to the presence of the street market. They even wanted private parking. This presence encouraged independent coffee shops and fancy bakers to flock in, driving a 'cupcake' revolution. When McCartney closed her studio there, so many other hopes were also extinguished.

While not a Council estate, the then Kensington Housing Trust (KHT) estate of Wornington Green, at the northern end of Portobello Road, was the first post-war estate in the borough to be targeted for development from 2006, as mentioned in Chapter 3. This had enthusiastic support from the Council, who saw the doubling of homes with private homes as a positive first step in their aspirations to 'improve' the demographic mix in North Kensington.

The supposed consultation process was deplorable. My first meeting with the KHT development team set the tone. Their presentation set out four options. I asked, 'Why are you bothering? You clearly want Option 3: bulldoze everything and rebuild.' The development manager looked intently at me and, with a faux-honest expression, promised to be 'open, honest and upfront'. He wasn't. A further consultation event took place in a marquee in Athlone Gardens, the beautiful park they were planning to destroy. As you entered the marquee, the Option 3 display board was in front of the entrance, brightly lit, slightly larger, with a smiling officer standing in front of it. I challenged her. 'Aren't you ashamed to call this a consultation?' I asked. She admitted that she was. I later found the KHT Board minutes, which laid out their plan to give their preferred option a prominent, brightly lit position with larger display boards, right opposite the entrance to the consultation.

The web of lies told by Kensington Housing Trust leading up to the planning application and eventual permission was mind-blowing. Apart from the first block where residents would have to be 'decanted' elsewhere, we were told, each block would be 'dropped' – an outrageous euphemism for the noise, dust and disruption of demolition – in turn and residents moved into a new one. Every resident would be rehoused on the estate in a home that was appropriate to their needs. We were told that it was essential to develop the estate as it was over 200 bedrooms short, and the new development would tackle this severe overcrowding. This was just not true. Some people were offered a move to Oxford by the 'honest' development manager I met, as if he was offering nirvana. But the bit of Oxford on offer was Blackbird Leys: at the time a notoriously crime-ridden estate on the outskirts, with very poor public transport links. At one all-day consultation I was told by a very self-satisfied officer that there had been 'no negative feedback'.

That was unsurprising, really, since I had been informed that not a single person had attended. Not one. So in fact there was 'no positive feedback' either. It was a gross misrepresentation. I called them out on this at a meeting. They were embarrassed but continued nonetheless, of course.

A major community campaign was held to save Wornington Green. One block, Pepler House, was declared a republic by its residents in 2009. Subsequently the whole estate was declared the 'United Estate of Wornington Green'. There was acres of press coverage, from local to national newspapers and TV, but all to no avail. The plans were approved, by one vote, at 1.45 a.m. at a Planning meeting. I was so angry that I had to be held down by two strong men to stop me (verbally) attacking the chair, who had exercised 'chair's discretion' and voted it through. This was totally against precedent, which deems that a split vote should be counted as a refusal.

The master plan, and detailed design for the first phase, was agreed, then the awful process of removing people from their life-long homes began, by a process that is difficult to see as anything other than dishonesty and bullying – some of which I personally witnessed. Some residents were offered 'special deals' on their rehousing packages, and told not to let anyone know. Of those who confided in me, these 'special deals' were the standard offer, boosted by some personal attention and flattery. An ex-employee of KHT reported on her blog that she was told to engage residents in 'a gentle game of tennis' – verbal that is – to encourage them to move out.

I watched the first phase of flats go up and was worried. I took a lot of photos. The first block and mews houses were so poorly constructed that they leaked: via internal plumbing, around the windows, from balconies, through roofs and even through walls.

There were at least two ceiling collapses and one floor collapse. After six years of trying to resolve snagging issues, in 2020 they were declared 'substantially' not fire-safe. Then landlord Catalyst Housing had to engage a waking watch, twenty-four-hour fire security guards – not due to flammable cladding but to badly fitted fire doors, a lack of fire breaks, and countless other issues related to abysmal workmanship. This action followed my demands to see the Fire Safety Assessment for the block, which took three months to produce. In this block, which had been partly funded by the Department of Communities and Local Government, there were seventeen Airbnb flats at last count. So much for it being a 'conservation area of the future' that would serve local people.

As well as social and Council housing that was in the firing line for 'improvement', there were numerous other sites around the borough awaiting development. In 2007 the Unitary Development Plan listed them: Kensal Gasworks; the electricity depot, Victoria Gardens; Newcombe House, Notting Hill Gate; Odeon Cinema, Ken High Street; three sites in Warwick Road; various sites within the Earls Court Exhibition Centre; Lots Road electricity-generating station; Kingsgate House, King's Road; various sites around Royal Brompton Hospital; the Iranian Embassy site in South Ken; Clearings I and II and the Denyer Street depot. All of these, apart from Denyer Street, were privately owned. Any Council committed to improve social housing could have bought some of these sites, or built social housing on the numerous plots of land it owned. I asked the Cabinet Member for Housing in November 2007 about this. She replied: 'There are not many sites just waiting to be developed into new social housing'. One of the many "blind spots". It's difficult to believe that she really believed this. With 9,000 households on the Housing waiting list, the Council was hell-bent on 'improving' property prices so they could 'build Labour out of the borough' as a Tory ally confided in me.

While discussing poverty in my ward in 2007, I joked to a Regeneration Sub-Group committee member, 'If we develop half the ward and double the number of residents with better-off people, it would halve poverty.' I was clearly being ironic. But their response was, 'What a good idea.'

In 2009, the Cabinet Member for Transport, Environment and Leisure (who by the time of the Grenfell Tower fire had become Leader of the Council) commissioned an Arts Strategy. The intention to 'develop a stronger and more sustainable creative economy' seemed perfectly rational, but the subtext was highly dubious: 'Cultural and recreational activity can contribute to neighbourhood renewal and make a real difference to health, crime, employment and education in deprived communities' and 'Using the arts as a tool for regeneration and consultation can help residents debate difficult issues and model the future.' It was clear to many of us that, rather than working to 'build community cohesion' the arts were to be mobilised to 'improve' some areas. Artwash, like 'greenwash', is a term used to describe the process of corporate reputation cleansing, by half-hearted or tokenistic interventions designed to make them appear socially empathic. An academic friend who had written his PhD on the issue of artwash told me: 'Artists are the shock troops of gentrification.' This process evolved spontaneously in some areas through displacement. That's different. I well remember the artists' squats in Shad Thames in the early 1980s when I lived in Bermondsey, where warehouse parties took place in these wonderful huge, empty spaces that were occupied by artists, musicians and other creative people. They were, of course, all evicted or otherwise squeezed out when developers bought the warehouses to convert into luxury flats. This Arts Strategy project was different, as it invited artists to occupy space at cheap rates and for a limited time to boost the 'bohemian' environment so loved by developers' marketing teams – the very people who would destroy the environment they were working on. The most repellent and toe-curling line in the Arts Strategy of 2009 was this: 'People see the north of the borough as having a hip, grungy, tolerant feel.'

People were poor. Some of these poor people were and are creative – musically, artistically. They were struggling. But the ambitions of the Council fed off their creativity, while the Council planned to displace them.

The ambition of this strategy knew no bounds. The role of the arts, it claimed, reduced 'inactivity', improved social inclusion and life quality, and reduced crime. In all seriousness, the strategy recommended setting up a local arts council. While this did not happen, over £2 million was – as we have seen – set aside to prop up the failing opera in Holland Park, maintain Leighton House, collect paintings of naked women for Leighton House, put art in parks, and support some – to my mind – utterly cringey performance art. All of these ideas were long-term commitments of the then Cabinet Member, so why we needed a strategy is beyond understanding. It would have been better, surely, to ensure that our own creative people could thrive here?

All of this was planned after the 2008 global financial crash when many residents were struggling to put food on the table, while they could see developer vultures circling their neighbourhoods. This project, in addition to founding a 'creative quarter', was to encourage local entrepreneurialism, which to many at the Council seemed to entail setting up a market stall or selling printed T-shirts or – the food of the gods – cupcakes. So many goddam cupcakes. Did cupcakes supplant art as the 'shock troops of gentrification', or was this a planned progression?

Alongside the wave of cupcakes, a number of proposals from academics and supposed think tanks were presented to the Housing Committee at the request of overexcited Tories. One such proposal in March 2007 was John Hills' 'Ends and Means: The future role of social housing in England', which was commissioned by the CLG. This paper contended that, due to a shortage of social housing and the accompanying tightened needs-based eligibility criteria, only the most vulnerable people would be able to access social housing. This polarised communities further. Hills stated the importance of social tenants having enough space at home to relax and study, and that overcrowding had a very poor effect on outcomes. He wanted housing providers to support tenants into work, or better-paid work, through skills training and other forms of support. He wanted more kinds of intermediate housing for people on middle incomes, and for tenants to be encouraged to save via a local credit union. He believed that people in private rented accommodation were often in worse situations than social tenants, but that social tenants 'complain more'. He also felt that it should be made easier to move within social and affordable housing, so that under-occupying households could downsize and overcrowded households could upsize.

Apart from having some blatantly paternalistic views, and a rather naïve hope that people on modest incomes would be able to save up for a mortgage deposit, Hills' view seemed relatively empathic.

Given that the dreaded 'stock options' appraisal to review the entire Council housing stock, was on the horizon, he agreed in principle that there should be a 'vision for the whole housing stock of the borough and how we will manage, enforce and enable in order to improve residents' quality of life and life chances'. He aspired to 'a decent home for all at a price within their means' and a 'move beyond the rationing approach towards an enabling approach'. He wished to 'create sustainable communities by allowing networks of family and friends to remain together' – an aspiration which, however well-meaning, was the last thing on the mind of the RBKC 'regeneration' team. As we will see, they took Hills' stark warning, inverted it and used it as the basis for their upcoming housing policy.

After the relatively 'softly, softly' Hills report, it became clear that the Council had more ambitious targets in mind for social housing in North Ken. A Stock Options Working Group was set up in 2006/7, just as I joined the Council, to review what was then seen to be an impending problem with the HRA – a potential deficit, which is illegal (it was later found to be 'erroneous'). Long-term options for Council housing stock were considered, with everything on the table from a total sell-off to partial development of estates to include money-making private homes, and infill.

The focus of these redevelopment plans soon became clear. Silchester West, with its extensive communal gardens, mainly low-rise and four high-rise blocks, plus Lancaster West, including Grenfell Tower and the finger blocks, were all in the firing line. The 'Notting Barns South master plan' was drawn up in 2009. However, the sums didn't add up, and it became obvious that this piecemeal approach would not address the supposed funding shortage.

After a very negative response from residents, the Council seemed to step back and looked at the wider implications of regeneration, such as a Hills-style focus on improving education, skills and life outcomes. At the same time, a review of potential HRA funding problems was less pessimistic. But by 2013, with the Tories in government and a change of Council leadership, the emphasis shifted back and attitudes hardened. The new Deputy Leader was given freedom to 'improve' North Ken, and proceeded to work with Planning and Housing officers and countless consultants in what felt like a full-on war against housing estates and social tenants, starting with Silchester.

Endless so-called public consultation meetings were held, meetings were held behind closed doors between senior Tory Councillors and officers, finances were juggled and options 'modelled'. A huge Stock Condition Survey concluded that the sum needed to bring Council housing up to scratch – £670 million over thirty years – was unattainable. Some of this was untrue. A whopping £30 million was calculated as being needed to repair Trellick Tower, when I knew that almost half that sum had already been spent. Estimates for work on the Tower were excessive: a friend who had worked for Goldfinger asked for a rival estimate for window replacement or repair, which was half the cost the Council was claiming. Heaven only knows how many other miscalculations the Council made to justify the wide-scale bulldozing and development of our Council estates. The sums were ambitious, to put it politely, and included roof and internal wall insulation of flats, many of which needed simply basic repairs. Thank goodness they didn't implement that programme, potentially using the flammable insulation materials for dry-lining walls and ceilings that they later used on Grenfell, despite – as we now know – plenty of advice to the contrary.

Around 2009 the Conservative Party under David Cameron, along with our local Tory Councillors, were licking their chops at the prospect of the upcoming general election alongside London local council elections in 2010. There was a notable swelling of macho excitement and egos around Kensington Town Hall, especially with three lively young Councillors who were possibly considering promotions that had been dangled before them: one of them was the future Deputy Leader responsible for the Grenfell Tower refurbishment. The prospects of a Conservative win at the general election mobilised them, and new ideas on the future of social housing came bursting forth.

A think tank, Localis, was commissioned by Hammersmith & Fulham Council Tory Leaders to come up with 'exciting, new' ideas. These were peppered with a frankly offensive narrative about social housing and its tenants. The Localis report was called 'Principles for Social Housing Reform'. A conference was held in mid-2009, which the Hammersmith & Fulham Tory Leadership attended with their counterparts from Kensington and Chelsea. They drank in every word, and apparently memorised the script. They came to Council meetings and regurgitated the language so often that I made a 'Tory cliché bingo' sheet. It kept me amused through a particularly turgid time. Their top clichés, absorbed at indoctrination sessions and spewed at appropriate moments, included 'broken society'; 'broken neighbourhoods'; 'dependency culture'; 'keeping focus in the face of a vociferous minority'; 'improving density'; 'barracks for the poor'; 'tightening criteria'; 'those in dire need'; 'culture of entitlement'; 'unlocking North Ken'; 'ghettoes for the poor'; 'welfare farming'; 'warehousing poverty' (bingo!). This was all to be tackled by the new Prime Minister's 'Big Society', whatever that meant.

This new lexicon was widely used in Council meetings and in the press.

In January 2010, in the run-up to the elections and seeing the way the wind was blowing, I proposed a motion to the Council committing to the social purpose of which social rented housing is a part. I asked the Council – in the light of proposals for the development of Wornington Green – to keep its promise to keep residents in the borough. I was told I was 'scaremongering', that I had 'no credibility in this chamber'. But I was also told this by another senior Tory Councillor: 'Write this down; we do not intend that residents should leave this borough.' The then Deputy Leader stated that my ward was a dung heap, and I wished to be 'queen of the dung heap'. The future Deputy Leader added that I represented 'a concrete ghetto for the poor, full of fear and paranoia'. We ensured that this insult was published prominently on the front page of the local paper, alongside a suitably unflattering photograph.

The thrust of the new government's approach to social housing would effectively break the pledge of responsibility to house low-income households, which was no longer seen as a public good. Proposals included cutting numbers of social rented housing stock to 'less than 10% of the nation's stock' (the total of Council and housing association homes comprise nearly one-third of all housing in RBKC); abolishing secure tenure; bringing social rent up to market value; tightening criteria so that only the most vulnerable would be eligible (counter to Hills' suggestions); replacing the 'duty to house' with the 'duty to advise'; and viewing Council estates as brownfield sites awaiting development.

Next door, in Hammersmith & Fulham, these proposals found their target: the then Leader declared, 'If we want to start knocking houses down, we will.' There were five estates on the list for bull-dozing and development. K&C followed where H&F led – and they were working closely with developers CapCo to demolish the Earls Court Exhibition Centre, while offering the neighbouring West Ken and Gibbs Green estate as a future 'brownfield site'. It would have been the biggest development site in London. They guaranteed to all Council residents that they could return to the new development, but these promises were discovered to be without foundation, to put it politely.

K&C Tory Councillors drew up target lists of estates and enthu-siastically took up the role of undermining and denigrating social tenants, implying that they were illiterate and workshy. Euphemisms abounded – they weren't socially cleansing, they were 'creating vibrant mixed communities in concentrated areas of deprivation'.

Another paper on social housing was written by Alex Morton of the Policy Exchange, a future member of Create Streets. His paper, 'Making Housing Affordable: A new vision for housing policy', was Think Tank Publication of the Year in 2010. Its premise was that house prices were high because there weren't enough new homes being built. So by unlocking the planning process, more homes would be available at all price levels. In 2010 the issue of over-supply of homes for private sale, enabling property banking and empty homes, had not been foreseen.

There were a number of proposals, most of which were com-pletely off-beam. The paper I kept from the time has scrawled on it 'The premise is wrong so the paper is wrong!' Various other 'solu-tions' were proposed, including: 'Reduce the rate at which rents/house prices rise by increasing the numbers of new homes built', suggesting that 'it is necessary to create a community-controlled planning system which moves to a more consensual model of planning, where those impacted by development [not local councils] decide on whether or not to allow development'. The next proposal was to 'Radically reshape the incentives social tenants face'. This proposed that 'needs-based' allocation should end, as it created a 'perverse incentive' not to increase income. Instead social housing should become a 'stepping stone' into ownership. Then we saw: 'Create a new Path to Ownership model of social housing and build more social homes . . . if home ownership is more affordable, social housing demand will dwindle'. This could apparently be done 'at almost no cost'.

Further recommendations included selling off existing stock on the open market. Somehow this was supposed to 'reduce welfare dependency for social tenants'. Along with comments from the then coalition partners Nick Clegg and David Cameron, these proposals came straight from the Localis bible, along with the conclusion that 'Social housing is currently exacerbating expensive problems of welfare dependency and poverty.'

This condescending, judgemental paper blamed social housing tenants for their perceived failure not to be rich, implying that all they needed was the incentive to earn more – by not allowing them to live long-term in social housing. So-called evidence in this paper included a link made between unemployment and social housing, which concluded that because more people who are unemployed live in social housing than in private housing, their housing has *caused* their unemployment – a total torturing of the co-existence vs causation debate. Other conclusions were: 'Localism that does not strengthen NIMBYs and involves the community is needed', forgetting that 'the community' are the very people concerned with what is being built in their backyard. And 'True localism would bypass NIMBYs and take more account of the majority view in most areas.'

The model for the brave new world proposed by this paper was Poundbury in Dorset, which had been built on land owned by the Prince of Wales by architects he had chosen. It was a huge Noddy's toytown of varied housing types – which I hear are poorly constructed and ageing badly. This new town was favoured by wealthy retired people rather than families, and a recent study has revealed that as the population has aged, the lack of low-cost housing and poor transport links have led to a shortage of home care workers, who were becoming essential.

Poor planning – and a perfect example of 'decision-based evidence-making'.

As the Localism Green Paper dragged its feet through parliament, promising far better local consultation processes and neighbourhood forums alongside the probable decimation of social housing due to lack of funding (and 'workshy' social tenants), RBKC continued its funding of big projects. In 2010/11 £80 million was set aside for the development of Holland Park School, £26 million to pimp Exhibition Road and £23 million to refurbish Kensington Town Hall offices. RBKC was clearly not short of funds.

One of the most fallacious and ultimately destructive policies of RBKC Council was its promotion of the 'fantasy' Crossrail station at Kensal Gasworks. This huge site of the former gasworks at the northern end of Ladbroke Grove had been subject to a master plan with Peabody Housing in 2005/6, just as I was campaigning to join the Council. Architecturally, the plan was fine. However, when you looked in detail at the breakdown of housing types, it was not. There were to be, at that time, 700 homes on the site adjoining the gasholders. Of these 700, one-third would be social housing for Peabody. But when I asked how many of these houses would be allocated to people on the RBKC waiting list, the story was alarming. Just sixty-seven of the new homes on the huge development site in the vastly overcrowded North Ken would be for K&C social tenants! We had quite a row about this, which the Council did their best to suppress. In the end, the Health and Safety Commission report on the Buncefield gas explosion in 2005 banned any housing from being built in close proximity to gasholders. The project was put on hold until the gasholders had been decommissioned. They were finally taken down in 2021, when the feeding frenzy began again.

Throughout these years the Council had maintained the myth that Crossrail, which passed the site to the south, would have a station at the gasworks – or 'Portobello Crossrail', as the Council liked to call it (even though it was some distance from Portobello Road). Yet we Labour Councillors had been told many times by Crossrail that building a new station here was physically impossible – or at least complex, insanely expensive, and too close to the next station along the line at Old Oak, which would be far better connected with the West London line and possibly HS2. The Labour Group lobbied for years to have a Plan B for the gasworks, so that there would be a fast transit connection from there to Old Oak but the Council refused to give up their fantasy, and the option for this connection was lost forever once work began on Old Oak. When I was MP, I met the chair of Crossrail in 2018 and asked him: 'When shall I buy my hat for the opening of the Portobello Crossrail station?' He laughed uproariously and said 'Never.'

Nonetheless, between 2006 and 2019 the Council spent £1 million or more on 'feasibility studies' to keep the lie alive. Year after year, new studies were commissioned showing in great detail how this fantasy station would fit into future schemes. At one point the station was estimated to cost £30 million, due to the need for a single long platform constructed with a bridge from the gasworks. This cost, of course, could have covered the developers' S106 contribution and eliminated the need for any social housing whatever on the site. So the housing would be for private tenants only!

While the Council used the fantasy station to push for a huge rise in property values in North Ken with this plan, it was continually flagged as a future transport link for new developments in the area. In 2018 I met some leaseholders of the Grand Union Centre, a new commercial and mixed housing development just across the road from the gasworks. They had paid a premium for their homes, believing that a station would be built there in the future. I checked the website marketing their homes – it was still maintaining this fallacy. I objected, and eventually mentions of the fantasy station were removed – too late, of course, for those who had already paid inflated prices for a home there.

The site *was* used for some time as a worksite for Crossrail – a final indignity, as the tracks bypassed K&C entirely. The gasholders were decommissioned and the site cleared, and yet another round of planning commenced in 2020. This time a possible 3,500–5,000 homes were planned. No station, no improved transport facilities ('We can get the buses to do a loop'), and the possibility of a footbridge over the wide railway tracks were suggested to 'link' 8,000–10,000 residents with the number 316 bus – and eliminate the chance of sufficient social housing, due to a lack of money once a bridge had been paid for. A potential density of 400 people/ hectare – more than double any other area in the borough – would be served by a criminally poor transport infrastructure of already overcrowded buses.

In 2013 the Leader of the Council met the Transport Minister, who informed him (to no one's surprise) that this new station did not have the support of either the Department for Transport or the Mayor of London. The Leader stated: 'The reasons for that lack of support remain frustratingly unclear.' Not to most of us, however! He then said that the Department for Transport would 'be glad to work with us on alternatives that might include some form of Heathrow-style monorail' – the proposal that the Labour Group had made some years before. But they had left it too late. Despite this, he concluded that 'the fight for our station must go on'. And indeed it did, with 2021 draft proposals under new Council Leadership for the site repeating the nonsensical possibility of a Crossrail station on site, despite Crossrail being essentially finished at this point, and with yet more Council taxpayers' money spent on 'feasibility planning'.

In May 2013, after a series of controversies, the Leader of the Council was replaced by one of the protectors of Leighton House. There was also a new Deputy Leader who was to lead the battle for North Ken, planning to develop all social housing estates, one by one. Battle lines were drawn. In my opinion, it would be no exaggeration to say that the election of this Leader and Deputy Leader lit the blue touchpaper that, four years later, set the fire at Grenfell Tower.

The Deputy Leader was a committed developer – and, to some people, a social engineer. His own development business was of the type that supported the Noddy's toytown of Poundbury and its pastiche neo-classicism that served no one but the developers' marketing team: a world of children with red balloons, hipsters on bikes, and cupcakes for the ladies. He announced early on that: 'North Kensington is the future South Kensington' as he planned to bulldoze an estate next to Ladbroke Grove and replace it with a terrace inspired by the white stucco terraces of South Ken, but with two or three storeys added to boost profit. The houses were mean, poorly designed internally, and definitely not aimed at the existing local population.

The Deputy Leader had swallowed the Localis approach whole. No estate was safe. He pushed forward plans for Silchester, promoting a high-density plan that had high-rise flats right next to the Westway (clearly for social tenants), communal gardens hardly worthy of the name (small and in shade for much of the day), and of course, 'reinstating the former grid pattern' of roads, which is a euphemism for market homes having front doors and a space to park on the street. As far as local people in Latimer were concerned, the master plan was almost universally loathed.

This assault on social housing was coming from various angles. We were very afraid that proposed Tory cuts would enforce our poorer neighbours to migrate out of the borough to 'low demand' (cheaper) areas, or even out of London. In the run-up to the local and general election we were accused, yet again, of scaremongering.

However, PM Cameron and his enabler Deputy Nick Clegg opened their term with Chancellor Osborne's austerity plan. Everything was to be cut, and housing welfare was top of the list. In September 2010 a shocking paper came to the RBKC Housing Committee – I will never forget it. Paper A6 was entitled

'Proposed Changes to Housing Benefit, Local Housing Allowance and Temporary Accommodation Subsidy'. I read it open-mouthed. After a detailed explanation it concluded: 'The potential for central London and the Royal Borough to effectively become a residential no-go area for anybody on a low income looking to rent is real . . . [including] long-standing families who may have lived in the borough all their lives.' Just what we had been afraid of.

We remonstrated with the Council, but the Cabinet Member for Housing was unrepentant: 'People will have to move to find alternative homes that they can afford.' In committee the Tory chair referred to this 'movement of families' as a means to 'achieve social goals', which we found were to 'engineer mixed communities'.

So they finally admitted their social engineering.

It was around this time that a reference to 'the Property Board' found its way into committee papers. I'd never heard of it, but it seemed to be leading on 'strategic property schemes and issues'. I asked for Board papers. They were denied me. I put in an FoI. Again, it was denied due to 'confidential commercial information'. I was eventually sent a Terms of Reference setting out the role and ambitions for this opaque 'Board', but the actual business of the secretive Board we didn't know existed were never shared. At this point there was a complete rearrangement of Property Services within the Council, bringing in new and more development-hungry management. This would bring Property Services from all the business groups under one department, and the leadership's plans to fruition. We were told it would be 'completely transparent'. It wasn't.

Not for the first – or last – time, a Council employee wrote to me anonymously to share their fears about this amalgamation; they feared they would lose their job if they spoke out publicly. They challenged the whole process of change in the Property Services department, particularly the huge waste of funds due to the use of 'change managers', who charged 'excessively'. This piece of work had been written in the period 2009/11 by an outside organisation that was named. The employee stated that, due to these changes, the Council was treating its staff very poorly and the so-called cost-saving exercise was driven by ideological reasons and to boost the career of certain individuals. The Council's new approach to property had 'made our lives a misery', with staff members left 'frazzled'. And so it continued.

I visited the new team with a colleague and a long list of questions. We were made very unwelcome. We left with heavy hearts, but on high alert.

Poor housing is bad for your health. This is a fact, about which there is a great deal of research. Children living in temporary accommodation suffer educationally and are three times more likely to suffer from poor mental health. Research by the National Health Service (NHS) and the National Housing Federation proved this in 2016.

Over the years the Council got away with moving people out. In 2011 there were four small schemes out of the borough that had either been developed or bought by the Council to house residents from the waiting list. But there is far more to this story. It seems – and let's hope this is a terrible misunderstanding – that there *is* Council-owned land destined for development, which they have no intention of building social housing on. The reason for this, very sadly, is likely to be a mix of cupidity and gerrymandering. In 2010, in a fiercely fought by-election caused by the resignation of a Tory Councillor who had become mixed up in a scandal relating to images of child abuse, Labour almost won a Council seat in Chelsea Riverside, losing by a measly nineteen votes. And in 2017 I shocked the Council and numerous others by winning the parliamentary seat of Kensington by twenty votes. Labour and Labour-friendly voters just need to see a viable alternative.

So, since they believe that social housing automatically equals Labour votes, there is no way on God's earth that the Tory-dominated Council will allow one single additional social housing unit to be built in what is now Chelsea Riverside ward. Yet there are numerous pockets of land and properties destined for development, mostly along Lots Road, which would be excellent sites for social housing. That's a great deal of land potentially for social housing. Land the Council insists it does not have.

Breaking this figure down was interesting. The overall estimate implied that all costs would be charged to the TMO, and excluded re-charges to the 2,493 leaseholders. The figure excluded rental income over that period. While it included £8.3 million costs for 'disability adaptations', it ignored the numerous grants available, including those under Labour's multi-billion-pound Decent Homes Programme. It included items which, though laudable, were not strictly speaking essential or even practical, such as double glazing for all properties, sound insulation, insulation including dry-lining internal walls and unspecific 'energy conservation', totalling £47.8 million. A further £50.9 million was set aside for 'improvements', which of course cannot be recharged to leaseholders.

Altogether, some very creative accounting was involved in this scaremongering exercise, which was clearly designed to encourage Councillors to vote for a housing stock transfer – most likely, sale to a housing association – to avoid having to make these repairs and to hand over responsibility for all social tenants to an outside body. The ultimate 'outsourcing' exercise, which for once did not take place.

Also that year, a huge backlog of repairs was 'discovered', and 1,482 homes failed the Decent Homes Standard. From my casework at the time, I knew that much of this was due to poor standards of workmanship and sometimes cheap and substandard materials used, including brand-new sanitaryware and kitchen equipment.

In short, vultures were circling over our Council housing.

Alongside this – which I didn't spot at the time but fills me with retrospective dread – was a section in the Stock Condition Survey report relating to 'trickle transfer', the slow transfer of property by selling it into the private sector. This looked at 'options for voids, community property and garages' as well as investigating 'leasehold transfer' and 'transfer of assets for use as temporary accommodation'. These properties were to be sold for profit, not to house homeless people.

A further report from Savills in April 2013, called 'Investing in our Housing Stock', praised the Tory government's reforms on 'self-financing' which 'enabled councils to review their long-term financial outlook'. Savills conducted an 'Asset Performance Evaluation', conveniently singling out 'low-performing' estates and blocks and lining them up for potential development. Alongside this, there was a totally unconscionable proposal to bring housing stock up to 'Kensington Standard' – a standard the Council might regret having such high hopes for, given what happened four years later. The clear aim at the time was to reduce the number of social rented homes, to raise rents, and pack more deprived areas with better-off people which would nudge statistics, but not improve lives. My feelings on this poured out in a blog I wrote at the time, which summed up the mood of the moment: 'Dear poor people, go away and stop depressing property prices'.

While the Council was struggling to find a way for TMO to achieve its goal of 'Kensington Standard' when so many of the homes it owned weren't even Decent Homes Standard, in July 2013 a battle raged in the Cabinet and among Councillors from both main political parties about the rising cost of the Holland Park School development. It had been planned to be 'the best school in England' by the then Leader of the Council. It was certainly going to be the most expensive. The original cost – £60 million – had already been superseded a few times and costs seemed to be spiralling out of control. But this was the Leader's pet project, nothing would stop him.

At the September meeting of the Audit and Transparency Committee that scrutinises Council spending and performance in great detail, concerns were raised about the 'ambitions' of the Council's Capital Programme which, under the control of Corporate Property, also seemed to be getting out of control. It was flagged up as a concern under the Risk Management table due to the sheer number of projects the Corporate Property team was responsible for. In June 2011 there had been eight projects underway: now there were thirteen, and many more being planned. The Director of Corporate Property stated with great confidence: 'Corporate Property is aiming to ensure that it gets things right first time, with rigour, scrutinising as it goes along, and putting in checks and balances in order to minimise risk.'

In 2014 the Housing and Property Scrutiny Committee was subjected to a presentation on 'Create Streets' by Nicholas Boys

Smith, which he called 'the case for normal terraced streets of houses and flats'. Precisely what 'normal' was to Boys Smith became obvious very quickly. His position was that, given the number of people who were unemployed, deprived, and prone to crime on high-rise estates, the architecture was clearly to blame. Never mind that people on low or no incomes are often allocated poor-quality housing and have no choice in the matter. He then compared these problematic estates with Prince Charles' Poundbury. He said that 'normal' streets such as these were popular. So yes, people would rather be rich than poor. The association was tenuous and very revealing of his personal preferences. He showed no evidence for a positive future for social housing.

But the 2014 local elections brought an earth-shattering (for some) result in Hammersmith & Fulham: Labour won. The previous Tory Council, with its Localis and RBKC cohorts, had been planning massive, far-reaching developments across the borough, including bulldozing the estates at West Kensington and Gibbs Green, which neighboured the H&F part of the humungous Earl's Court site. The new H&F Labour leadership threw itself into overturning many of these plans, and pledged to save West Ken and Gibbs Green estates.

Meanwhile, Corporate Property had been sniffing around the Warwick Road estate, a hidden but rather lovely estate built on top of Council offices on Pembroke Road with a central garden, very family oriented. It was designed by Arup Associates. But the diagnosis was clear: 'full development is best'. The Council committed to buy out thirty-four leaseholders at full market price – plus a bit.

At around this time, the government was proposing planning reforms, including permitted development rights (PDRs) to change designated office space to residential and to make this reform permanent. Mayor Johnson had apparently previously said that he would use 'thermonuclear weapons' to prevent this change, but he did not. The London Assembly called Mayor Johnson out on his failure to keep to his word.

The Westway Trust, which manages the 23 acres under the Westway flyover for the benefit of the community (in compensation for the mass destruction required to build the flyover) was losing its social purpose at this time: it had made plans for a major development, including high-end shops, cafes, a food market and housing, right next to the heavily polluting Westway. The plans included nothing to serve the needs of the local population. The Westway Trust director led this plan with an article in the local paper headed 'Cultural focus pays rich dividends'. Early visuals for the project, aside from enraging residents with the project's clear intention to gentrify the area, included not one person of colour or older person.

These plans would have closed the stables towards the west of the Trust-managed land – stables that cater for inner-city children as well as young disabled people. There was an outcry. Eventually the plans were shelved. But the Council-run Maxilla Children's Centre did not survive the cull, and closed. Westway Information Centre, which housed the then Citizens Advice Bureau, was developed and leased to a private nursery, and a Pret sandwich bar added at street level.

It wasn't just North Kensington residents who were up in arms. In June 2015, Chelsea residents paraded down King's Road to protest against proposals for a Crossrail station at the corner of Sidney Street and King's Road, and in October 2015 the good people of Chelsea signed a huge petition to save the Victorian school building at Marlborough School, and even came to protest at a Council meeting.

September 2015 saw four more projects added to the potential bulldozing list. Raddington Road and Oxford Gardens had two blocks end-on to Portobello Road – clearly a site too good to waste on Council tenants. A row of two-storey blocks on Portland Road and a row of houses on Elgin Mews were also slated for the same treatment.

All these schemes were pitched by the Cabinet and the Town Clerk as part of the RBKC Efficiency Plan. This would create 'an attractive, safe and diverse area'. They insisted they were 'listening to our residents . . . championing their interests' and of course 'taking actions and decisions that are transparent and well explained'.

The sale of Thamesbrook Residential Care Home was finally completed in early 2016, for £75 million. Plans for a 'bigger, better library' which would restore the Victorian building – clearly deemed unsuitable for its built purpose – and hand it over to a private prep school romped ahead. To tackle a growing campaign against leasing this Victorian masterpiece, which had been built by public subscription, the Director of MediaComs stated he would 'carpet-bomb North Kensington' with leaflets supporting it. A master plan for Silchester East and West, as a 'conservation area of the future', was being presented, which would 'provide new affordable homes, especially for those on ordinary incomes'.

'Normal' streets for people on 'ordinary' incomes.

In April 2016 the Cabinet agreed to buy a local further education college for £25.6 million. This was done without consultation, without anybody's knowledge, and deliberately (as we later discovered) keeping local Councillors in the dark.

£25.6 million. Without consultation. With impunity.

In October 2016 the Council bought a property adjoining the soon-to-be-bulldozed Balfour Burleigh estate, a beautiful former mortuary building, for £8.6 million. It was to be developed for private renters only. A site was bought in Park Royal to move the car pound from Lots Road, clearing the site for development; a 'delivery strategy' for the Edenham site in front of Trellick Tower was put together; the Denyer Street depot was sold for £12 million. There are many such examples.

Meanwhile, the construction of the secondary school on Lancaster Green, Grenfell Tower's amenity space, led the residents of the Tower to demand a very long overdue refurbishment. As we now know, RBKC spent as little as possible on this refurbishment, which was beset by problems. After the fire, the incoming RBKC chief executive officer said what we had all been thinking: that the Council had behaved like 'a property developer masquerading as a local authority'.

Chapter 5

THE SURPRISE MP

Labour Party colleagues had occasionally suggested that I should consider becoming an MP. I had always said no, for a variety of reasons. Some years back I thought that, as my children were young and I had no family backup, fulfilling my domestic responsibilities while being an MP would be impossible. In addition, I only wanted to stand somewhere I had an allegiance to. At a stretch that could have been Bow, as I was born at Mile End Hospital, though I'm not familiar with the area. Then there was Kensington. We all knew that Kensington would be a waste of time and effort, as we could never win this true-blue, favoured-by-the-government constituency. I also had work as a freelance journalist and researcher that I enjoyed and that I could fit around my children. In addition to this, I was halfway through a PhD. Did I want to change things?

Over the years I worked more on campaigning in the local party, and in the 2015 general election I was campaign coordinator. I threw myself into the role, did the sums, followed the predictions, helped select our candidate, worked on the manifesto, designed the literature, and did a lot of door-knocking. With an excellent candidate and a good campaign – in a terrible year for Labour – we knocked six points off the Tory vote.

After the disastrous Brexit referendum result in 2016 and the resulting public loss of confidence in the Prime Minister, there were mutterings about a possible general election. I was vaguely considering sacrificing six months of my life to 'give the Tories a scare', as I saw it, when I was approached by an unlikely source. There are quite a few residents' associations around the wealthier parts of K&C who knew me from Planning Committees, when I had always done my best to listen, to consider carefully, and to vote independently (I was told by a former Whip that the Tories were often whipped into making decisions favourable to developers in Planning Committee – which is illegal). Anyway in late 2016 I was contacted by a member of a residents' association for 'a chat'. I was a bit worried, and told a colleague about it in case I disappeared into Toryland, and assured them I would bring a long spoon to sup with them. Over the years other colleagues had 'gone rogue' when they had spent too long in the presence of socialising Tories; they forgot their politics. I have no problem with being friendly, but keep your politics true.

When I met this person, this is what they told me: 'Our current MP is a useless Brexiter. We know you're a Remainer, and we know you and like how you stand up for residents. If you stand for Labour in the general election when it comes, a lot of us will vote for you.'

Well, I hadn't expected that. I talked to family and colleagues, who were supportive. We had very little time for the usual selection process when the election was announced, and in the end my application was blessed by the Labour Party National Executive Committee. I was a Councillor of many years' standing, a hard worker, and had been Labour Group Leader on the Council, so I was a known entity.

There was little time for reflection. We just dived in. We had very carefully written literature that detailed my take on Brexit (remain in the single market and customs union for starters), some of which wasn't specifically Labour policy at that time, though it was eventually. We used nice photos and included courteous explanations – nothing flashy, nothing shouty, and all true. Local candidates have the edge at general elections. While the incumbent MP was also local, she was not popular, and of course she was a Brexiter, in a constituency that voted 70% to remain in the EU.

I was pleasantly surprised to find support where I hadn't expected it. I was known; you can't buy that personal vote. There was a huge team of local parents I'd known forever through nursery, primary school, Cubs, ballet classes and mums networks such as book clubs. A dedicated team and hundreds of supporters leafleted, door-knocked, talked to their neighbours and campaigned tirelessly. It must be said that some of my Council colleagues thought it ridiculous, and couldn't take seriously any kind of election campaign in Kensington. They told us off for time-wasting and spent their time in neighbouring constituencies that they felt were under threat.

While we were getting a positive response, a month ahead of the election we still didn't consider that we'd actually win. Then a friend told me, 'Ignore the polls, check the bookies – you're ahead'. To my surprise, I was.

At this point, several friends and family members bet on me to win.

Polling day was extraordinary. The atmosphere was electric, everyone was mobilised to get out the polling-day cards, door-knock, drive people to polling stations, and ensure that everyone had voted. There was a brief respite, then it was down to the Town Hall. Everyone was nervous and edgy. The usual camaraderie between parties, which was present when there was no likelihood of political change, was absent. Bizarrely, the Conservative candidate was nowhere to be seen.

The first count came in at around 1.30 a.m. I'd won by fifty-seven votes. The horrified Tories demanded a full recount. The second count came at around 4 a.m. I'd won again. A bundle count, where bundles of fifty votes are sorted into political parties, was demanded. By that time the counters were falling asleep at their tables, and we were all sent home to sleep. My head was spinning. We returned on Friday evening at 6 p.m.

By the time we returned, there had been a huge turnaround in Labour's fortune across the country, with numerous new MPs being elected. But Kensington? The press were gathered outside the Town Hall along with a large group of supportive residents, singing, chanting and drumming, creating a festival atmosphere. It was amazing.

There was a deadly hush in the Great Hall as the count recommenced. We'd called for reinforcements and had been joined by the Leader and Deputy Leader of Hammersmith & Fulham Council, Councillor colleagues from Tower Hamlets and Westminster, and a Labour Party lawyer who came to oversee proceedings. He schooled us thoroughly. We had strict instructions on how to conduct ourselves, how to monitor the count, how to deliberate on spoilt or uncertain ballots. You could cut the atmosphere with a knife. The press were twitching outside and in the public gallery, and there were constant messages on my phone and my agent's phone.

We were, for that evening, the number-one news story.

Around 9.30 p.m. the vote was called. Labour had won by twenty votes. Twenty! I read out my hurriedly composed acceptance speech, which included the words:

Thank you for the painstaking work carried out on our behalf by the Liberal Democrat candidate and her team for picking off some of the disaffected Tory vote. And thanks to the disaffected Tories who didn't take that step, but voted for me.

A bit cheeky, I know.

The Town Hall erupted. Our supporters outside were euphoric, shouting, 'Our MP! Our MP! Our MP!'. I was laden with flowers, hugs, kisses. I was handed a mike. Generally I'm not good at making spontaneous comments, but this came to me in a second: 'Kensington has spoken! Never be silent again!' A police officer winked at me and I was congratulated from all quarters. And a few brave punters in my team had just made a great deal of money.

After fielding numerous press comments, I eventually returned home with close family and a few friends, wanting a breather, but my home was invaded with well-wishers; there was no escape. I was told that all the pubs and bars in Portobello had erupted when the announcement came through, and people were celebrating in the streets. It was just incredible. Saturday and Sunday were packed with press interviews, and invitations flooded in from residents' associations and other groups to meet them. We did a victory walkabout around North Kensington; the response was amazing. My uni professor sent me congratulations, and we started the process to suspend my PhD research. Friends came forward to volunteer their help to set up an office. It was all so unexpected, it was giddying.

Then it was Tuesday 13 June. I went to bed, exhausted.

Helicopters woke me.

Chapter 6

GRENFELL

Four days after I was elected as MP for Kensington, in the early hours of 14 June 2017, I awoke to the sound of helicopters. This isn't unusual in North Kensington – usually it means that someone has stolen a car and is being followed by the police – but this time was different. There was more than one helicopter, and it didn't stop. I was confused. Eventually I turned on the radio and heard the news: a tower block in North Kensington was on fire. I leapt out of bed – then found myself running down the road. At some point, I checked that I was dressed. Incredibly, I was wearing clothes and shoes, and had my bag, keys and phone with me. I have no recollection of getting dressed and leaving the house – none whatsoever. I ran down St Helen's Gardens, under the Westway, down Kingsdown Close. As I reached the Methodist church in Lancaster Road, the scene of horror revealed itself. There were people crying, holding each other, looking desperate, their eyes pleading with me. There were journalists there too, who recognised me and wanted to interview me. They later recalled my first impressions on seeing the fire, and my comments.

I have never talked about what I saw or heard that morning, and I probably never will. I can't imagine who it might help; it would certainly not help me to put it into words. Just writing about it, skirting the facts as I am now, triggers flashbacks I have no wish to revisit. Suffice it to say, it scarred my soul forever with a fury I cannot put into words. And I will never forgive those who were responsible.

I walked around the neighbourhood, visiting rescue centres to see how they were coping, for much of the morning. A lot of people greeted me eagerly, as if they thought I would know how to help them. It was mortifying. Throughout that day I saw just two Council officers. One was helping at a rescue centre: he was there because he lived nearby and had rushed to help in a personal capacity. Another was a housing officer, who spent that day and the days after on the phone, trying to find temporary accommodation for hundreds of newly homeless, traumatised and bereaved people. Some had family members who had lived in Grenfell Tower but had disappeared: these people didn't know if their relatives were dead or were being cared for in hospital somewhere. Some people spent days driving around hospitals looking for family members and friends. Not all were successful.

One of the scenes I do remember is seeing the Leader and Deputy Leader of the Council being interviewed for TV in front of the blazing tower, with people burning to death behind them, saying, 'We offered them sprinklers and they turned them down.'

A. Blatant. Lie. The first of many, no doubt. That was the only time I saw the Leader and Deputy Leader there, and I never saw the Chief Exec of the TMO. But I do know that, when they were asked afterwards, including at the Inquiry, why they didn't check that the emergency plan was being followed and that officers were being mobilised, they said they had been 'too busy talking to the press'.

I have no words.

The scene of utter chaos on the ground – the lack of organised help, the free hand given to vulture journalists – was unforgivable. By the end of the week, London Gold Command – the emergency services team responsible for major disasters – had taken over, and thank goodness for that. Offers of help from other councils across London, which had been refused for days, were at last accepted and coordinated, and a very slow, difficult response began. But the first few days of chaos had taken their toll and had a high cost. Senior officers and Councillors were sidelined by London Gold Command and eventually moved aside – or sacked. And so they should have been. One was allegedly marched out of the Town Hall by police after refusing to resign and leave the building.

I remember parts of those first days in agonising detail, and parts I have no memory of at all. I have since been asked, why didn't I help people at one centre or another? I don't know if they thought that, since I was now an MP, I could walk into an office with phones, staff and funding immediately at hand. None of that was the case. At first, it was just me. Then the Party Leader's office sent help. But when you enter parliament you are on your own: you have to fight even to get an office and a landline. I worked with fantastic volunteers all summer in my MP's office before I had time to take on staff.

How, then, did it all come to this?

I joined the Board of the Kensington and Chelsea TMO in 2008 – not because I was especially keen to do this, but because it was considered useful to understand how our Council housing was run

– and frankly the Councillor who had been on it previously had had enough. From the earliest days, it was very trying. Some of the other Board members were tribal, to put it politely, and were not keen to have anyone at the table who would ask awkward questions. I read all the papers before meetings – and I had plenty of questions. There were ongoing rows between some Board members and staff members; meetings were poorly chaired; and it was no surprise to me that the organisation was not managing its properties properly, given the chaos at the top.

Some of the arguments were petty. Although non-Councillor Board members were paid an allowance, the 'hospitality' before meetings was lavish. Tables groaned with expensive nibbles, wraps, sandwiches and drinks. Hardly any were ever eaten. I asked what happened to them afterwards and was told, 'they are given to staff'. That's not a problem in itself, of course, but perhaps it's a signal of KCTMO's skewed priorities. Then there was huge excitement about the 'Board away-weekend'. This was to help Board members bond, over training and some meetings. It looked to me like a well-funded jolly, and the location looked like a castle. As we were discussing at meetings the possibility of raising rents and more tenants were falling into arrears every month, losing their jobs and security in the aftermath of the global banking crash and the government's 'austerity' programme of cuts to local government, the Board away-weekend seemed not only excessive but also tasteless and indefensible. I asked how many hours of training were involved, and was told it was around four hours. To give up a weekend, and arrange childcare for three whole days, I needed something more purposeful than that. I suggested we do the training on a Friday in London. Some members erupted with fury at the suggestion.

I was – not for the first or last time – screamed at by four Board members while the chair sat there smiling.

In the end we had the training in London on a Friday, in the Hilton Olympia, with lots of sandwiches and wraps. And some of the Board members hated me for it.

Tenants complained endlessly about the poor service and woeful response to repairs provided by the TMO, and they twice called extraordinary general meetings to discuss the failures of the organisation. The meetings were very heated. Police were called. Yet nothing seemed to get any better.

Having discussed the problems with the relevant senior officers at the Town Hall, it was eventually decided by legal officers to bring in an independent adjudicator to review the work of the TMO – particularly, but not exclusively, the complaints and repairs systems. The Memoli report came out in April 2009; it was explosive. In forty-seven pages it dissected the history, practice and failures of the TMO and its management, staff and Board. It listed complaints that had never been dealt with, and repairs that had been completed several times as they were so badly done. It looked at the chaotic charging and billing for leaseholders, some of whom had to pay for repairs that had never been undertaken, or had been charged twice for repairs that had been completed badly the first time around and that were still inadequate. Some of the stories of damp, mould, leaks and lack of heating were heartbreaking. The report made numerous recommendations for improvement.

Another section looked at the 'behavioural' aspects of communications between tenants and the TMO. The words 'malevolent', 'mistrust', 'malaise' and 'treated with contempt' were used of TMO staff, which the report put down to an 'unhappy culture'. There were instances of breach of confidentiality and a very careless attitude to data protection; one tenant was taking legal action against the TMO in relation to this.

A section on governance reviewed the functioning and practice of the Board itself, and concluded that training and reminders on confidentiality were needed, as several Board members had breached the TMO's Code of Conduct. Given the number and frequency of complaints about the quality of repairs and major works, the report wondered if the TMO was, in fact, incapable of finding reliable contractors.

A financial audit in December 2006 had reported innumerable problems with charging, billing, and with financial governance in general. There was a huge backlog in repairs, and a huge backlog in claiming arrears for rent, service charges and leaseholder bills. This was reviewed once again in 2009, when it was found that little had been achieved in the previous three years.

One of the conclusions of this report was: 'From the evidence gathered by the Adjudication Service, some residents are receiving substandard services . . . Furthermore, the residents expect an early response to the queries they raise without the need to keep chasing . . . There appeared to be little or no follow-up procedure'. The Memoli report was referred to several times at the Inquiry.

An Improvement Plan was set in place, with thirty-four recommendations covering all areas. It made little tangible difference, though a – long-winded – process was put in place to find a new chief executive.

One of the estates that had suffered endless problems due to inadequate maintenance over many years was Lancaster West, which included Grenfell Tower. Despite huge local opposition, the Council was planning to build a sorely needed new secondary school on the green space in front of Grenfell Tower, Lancaster Green, and to rebuild the leisure centre next to it. The Green was the amenity space for the Tower – part of the rationale for tower-block living is to have green space outside, but the Council saw this as 'wasted' space. As the plans progressed, the complaints from local residents, RAs and groups grew. Why was the Council spending tens of millions of pounds on a new building on the Tower's amenity space while ignoring the endless complaints and appalling state of repair of Lancaster West and the Tower? Lifts broke down regularly, gaps around the windows let in wind and rain, and the boiler often broke down, leaving residents without heating or hot water for days on end.

After endless rows, meetings, negotiations, emails and letters, the Council finally agreed to refurbish Grenfell Tower. When they had a general idea of what would be done – which included new windows, new boilers and new lifts – residents were pleased. A senior Tory, very pleased that they had finally 'tamed the beast' and reached agreement of a kind, asked me if I would endorse this decision. In October 2012, as I was leaving the KCTMO Board after an exhausting, stressful four-year stint on it, I wrote a few lines in support of the project.

I have had cause to regret the decision to endorse the refurbishment many times since, as it was leapt upon by malevolent political forces trying to implicate me in the Council's choice of flammable cladding and insulation on the Tower – decisions that were made in later years by other people. In the days after the fire, I was publicly accused, in the press and on social media, of having 'signed off the cladding'. I received death threats, and was offered police protection.

My Councillor successor on the TMO Board was a witness at the Grenfell Tower Inquiry, at which she related how she was harassed, undermined and eventually 'bullied off the Board' for bringing up residents' concerns. Interestingly, the Conservative Board member who was there before, during and after the fire had no such intimidation or hate directed at her, and neither did the other Conservative member who served on the Board at the same time as me. At the time of writing, that Conservative former Board member is the Leader of the Council.

Prior to the fire, I was also on the Housing and Property Committee and the Planning Committee. At none of these meetings was there ever any discussion of the implications of the choice of one kind of cladding and insulation over another, and neither should there have been. Councillors sitting on committees are not supposed to have that degree of technical knowledge. In addition, all the decisions on changing the cladding took place between planning officers and the Cabinet Member, away from the committee. This is all documented.

On Friday 16 June, two days after the fire, we heard there was to be a March for Justice. It was very hot: everyone was on the streets, especially the newly homeless, who were congregating to support each other. This was the point at which the former MP made a fleeting visit, then wrote to the Leader of the Council that people were behaving 'like gangs'. Clearly she feared civil unrest on the part of traumatised families who she regarded as savages. A lot of people were very angry, and quite rightly so. It was just before London Gold Command took over the response, and it was still complete chaos. I met families who were sleeping in their cars, or in the park. Some people were being refused access to rescue centres because they had no ID; they had lost everything. All of this was denied at the time, but has been revealed in the Inquiry to be accurate.

There were countless journalists, some respectful and others really not. I asked the Council to set up a verification system so that journalists would have passes and people would know if they were legitimate or just vultures; I never had a reply. Some journalists were shoving cameras into people's faces as they cried. One followed me down the street, repeating the nonsense that the previous MP had written in the *Evening Standard* about my 'responsibility' for the fire. A colleague of mine defended me, and was punched to the ground by the so-called journalist.

At one point a group of young men was gathering. They were being addressed by two community leaders. The atmosphere was twitchy. I dived into the centre of the group and was quickly introduced by the speakers, both of whom I knew well. I said a few words, to the effect of, 'Don't let the press write your narrative. Address your anger where it counts, not on the streets', and I can't remember what else. Whatever we said did help to calm the moment. Meanwhile, a Labour Party officer who had been sent to 'help' tried to drag me out of the crowd, implying that I had no place there. I refused to leave and explained that these were *my* angry people, and if he didn't understand that he should leave me be. Which he did.

In the days and weeks afterwards, I spent as much time as possible in the area visiting response centres, meeting Gold Command, feeding information back to them from the ground. Between that and trying to get my head around my place in Westminster, where I now knew that I had to fight for everything, including an office and phones, I barely slept.

My maiden speech in the House of Commons did not spare anyone. It was well received by those who counted. The journey had begun.

Given the inept, chaotic response to the fire and its aftermath, and the uncaring attitude to the bereaved, homeless and traumatised people it left behind, in July 2017 the government appointed the Independent Grenfell Recovery Taskforce. This Taskforce comprised four leading figures with varying and supposedly complementary skills in local government, housing and social care. Their role was to support, advise and guide the Council in the delivery of recovery, including rehousing survivors; addressing weaknesses in KCTMO; community engagement; ensuring those affected received 'cross-cutting' support; improving governance to tackle recovery; and ensuring that long-term plans for the site were developed with all parties, including the community.

In October 2017 the first report by the Taskforce was published, looking at the response in those crucial early days, weeks and months. It was damning. It opened with recommendations and a hard-hitting summary:

> RBKC failed its community on the night of 14 June and in the weeks following . . . RBKC was distant from its residents; highly traditional in its operational behaviours; limited in its understanding of collaborative working . . . and with a deficit in its understanding of modern public service delivery.

The report went on to outline four themes that needed focus: 'More pace; greater empathy and emotional intelligence; skills and training on how to work with a traumatised community; and innovation.' It noted that various actions that had been suggested to improve community engagement 'have not been delivered'. The Council needed to undertake a 'detailed mapping of its community so it can understand it better'. 'Improving support and empathy' was also noted as a priority. The final point related to the charred skeleton of the Tower, still uncovered after six months. Now it was a crime scene, as well as re-traumatising people every day: 'It is reprehensible that it has remained uncovered for so long.' Strong words.

This report then went into further detail about 'a severe trust deficit between the local community and RBKC', continuing that 'these failings . . . are still contributing to the current trust deficit'. A comment that 'Developing plans and reports . . . do not equate to making a difference to people on the ground' concluded that 'there is more that concerns us than we can take comfort from'. Commenting on plans to create a Grenfell Department, the report says: 'This may be an appropriate initial response, but looks expensive and therefore unsustainable in the longer term.'

During conversations between Taskforce members and the community, it emerged that they felt they had suffered from 'political neglect', and that their area had been a 'political blind spot' for the Council. However, the report said that:

The Taskforce has been highly impressed by the work of the various voluntary-sector agencies that responded to the immediate needs after the fire and have continued to respond to this day. Local individuals alongside various faith-based organisations, local, national and international aid charities, have come together to provide trusted support and relief, which deserve great praise. The Council now has the opportunity to learn from, harness and embed the social capital that has been created in the borough.

One of the organisations the report said that the Council could learn from was the mosque in Golborne ward, Al-Manaar, whose social programme outperformed many local voluntary organisations that were funded by the Council. The mosque opened its doors to everyone who had been affected by the fire – survivors, bereaved, neighbours – and gave them somewhere to sleep in safety; clothes; food; a play space for children; and, over time, counselling. Hundreds of people went there every day to get help of all kinds; no one was refused. The mosque literally saved lives and sanity. Yet the Council, to this day, sees Al-Manaar as an extension of local voluntary groups rather than what it is: a partner organisation carrying out work the Council still fails to provide.

The Taskforce also mentioned, after residents' comments about the chaotic response to the fire, that: 'The lack of coherent collaborative working across agencies is a long-standing weak point, which the Council allowed to fester unchallenged.' It noted a strong demand from residents for the Council to be brought into special measures, overseen by commissioners.

For many people, it was a huge relief to read this first report. It was precisely what so many people had complained of for years, but no one had listened. Would the Taskforce be the instrument of change that we all needed so desperately?

The second report by the Taskforce came six months later, in March 2018. It was unstinting in its praise for community action and organising: 'We have observed that there is a level of community spirit and attachment not often seen in local communities in London. A dynamic and diverse, yet disparate, mix of communities has, in the aftermath of 14 June, been forged together. . .' Once again, it proposed that the Council engaged with, worked with and learned from their example. However, the report noted that the Council was still not acting on the advice given in the Taskforce's first report: the Taskforce had 'not seen enough . . . converting plans into action, and delivery on the ground remains patchy'. The problem of the 'trust deficit' came up more than once. The report also noted that there were 'no complaints of lack of resources . . . [but] complaints of slow response' and 'unsympathetic or inappropriate responses from Council staff and Councillors'.

The report recommended that 'RBKC needs to develop a comprehensive recovery vision . . . with the local community, and it will require much more than the usual "consultation" . . . We have seen individual elements of recovery being driven forward separately in an uncoordinated fashion.' Once again the report underlined the need to work with the voluntary sector:

The Council needs to move beyond the historical grant-giving relationship and develop new and interdependent ways of working, where they listen more to those from the local community, the people who have the trust, confidence and credibility with the local community, and work with them to co-produce a way forward.

Instead, the report noted a continued practice of 'silo working' in the Council and 'little evidence to date of planning for longer-term social and economic support' that could build on the existing 'social capital' that they noted was in abundance elsewhere in the borough.

Some comments from residents were noted: 'We have not seen evidence of a change. We can see there is activity, but it's still not evident what is actually changing on the ground' and: 'There's been a shameful waste of resources . . . Money from government and donations is not getting to the people.' And some especially difficult comments: 'Someone from Care for Grenfell said, if you were really suffering you'd have called sooner' and 'It feels as though [the Council believes] there is a set period to grieve, and you get a set period of empathy, and this translates into a set period of what you're entitled to.'

The report then turned to performance against recommendations, stating that 'delivery of many services has been . . . variable but overall poor'.

The third Taskforce report came out in November 2018, and the fourth in June 2019. They both adopted a rather weary tone, since so many of the Taskforce recommendations had still not been implemented.

The third report stated: 'Too often RBKC makes avoidable mistakes that negate a lot of good work. We hear far too often of basic errors – for example, meetings that are not publicised until the day before, of essential emails that go astray and are not followed up.' It also underlined 'poor and insensitive management causing unnecessary and avoidable distress' and stated that: 'There is little evidence that the Council have systems in place that use the knowledge and intelligence of frontline staff to constantly improve how they deliver services.' This is particularly evident in the area of rehousing, which according to the report remains 'painfully slow', including a truly depressing number of sixteen households still in hotels, with the likelihood of them still being homeless for Christmas 2018.

While the Council had signed up to the Hillsborough Charter and committed to 'culture change', the Taskforce saw little change, and what there was deemed 'patchy':

> We believe there are pockets within the organisation who do not yet understand that the Grenfell tragedy is now the defining feature of RBKC, and that cultural change is required. We still hear on occasion that there is an expectation they will be able to return to business as usual once everyone has been rehoused.
>
> Everyone would have expected RBKC to be further on with this seventeen months on . . . [due to] the legacy of problems we highlighted in our previous reports – poor understanding of people's needs until relatively late in the process . . . While highlighting the 'acute shortage of larger family homes within the Council's own stock' they recommend 'a longer-term housing strategy for the borough'.

There had been more community engagement, but it wasn't necessarily better: 'Bereaved, survivors and residents are worn out by the many times they are "consulted" by RBKC . . . [but] the many different consultations being carried out by different sections of the Council is an indicator that it continues to work in silos.' Frustration was expressed when people were directed by the Council to its website for evidence of consultation: 'The overall look and approach remain old-fashioned: papers need to be concise, written in plain English, jargon-free and with the decisions up-front.' RBKC's external communication is poor: '. . . getting even the simplest things wrong, such as meetings and papers being publicised too late'. It ended with a damning indictment:

> In our view, RBKC have not yet made sufficient progress in recovery . . . we are still not seeing enough successful outcomes . . . we would [like to] see . . . a visible culture change across the Council where the values are not just words on a page but are brought to life in everything that RBKC do.

The fourth Taskforce report, in the form of a letter to the Secretary of State written in June 2019, gives no comfort whatever to these repeat offenders:

> We observe strategic weaknesses that concern us . . . RBKC is not yet achieving the level of performance in its recovery effort that we have consistently suggested they aim for; we are unconvinced that the current pace of change will achieve this in the foreseeable future.

While repeating several comments from the earlier reports, this letter comments on the 'continued frustration for local residents. . . We are unconvinced that the cultural change programme is having penetration'. In relation to the five-year £50 million Grenfell Recovery Strategy, the letter states: 'A lot of the programme is still to be developed in detail, with key performance indicators and tangible outcomes yet to be defined' and 'There is little in the strategy itself that explains how the Council will govern the programme and drive delivery'. The rehousing process at that date was progressing slowly, but 'The Council is still struggling to convert the high degree of social capital that is clearly apparent into a positive force.'

In a devastating analysis of community relations, the report goes on to state:

The quality of the Council's relationship with the local community in the north of the borough is inconsistent and too frequently weak. The Council have rightly focused their efforts on the bereaved and survivors. However, the relationship with the wider community in North Kensington has not made sufficient progress. In some respects, it is going backwards.

And it concludes:

In preparing this report we again asked ourselves . . . whether we can give you the assurance that this Council has the capacity and capability to drive forward delivery of a recovery. [. . .] These echoes of our first observations in 2017 have led us to conclude that there remain underlying problems within the Council's approach that still need to be addressed.

And the fifth, and final, report in March 2020 repeated the same concerns: lack of pace, lack of culture change, poor quality of relationship with affected people. All these issues were being articulated regularly by residents and those working on the frontline. In essence, the Taskforce was seeing through our eyes, yet still the Council did not recognise its failure or know how to change:

We remain concerned about the overall pace of change. Too often we have seen milestones being put back or taking longer than planned to deliver and the Council putting forward reasons why it cannot do something rather than what it will do . . . We would urge greater challenge from the senior leadership, where a 'can't do' attitude is expressed.

At this point the Council had abolished the Grenfell Recovery Scrutiny Committee (GRSC), which had been very effective. In a wave of activity they had changed the scrutiny system to that of Select Committees (at least, what they thought were Select Committees) and decided to absorb the various Grenfell-related issues in these overarching committees. Residents were furious. It was clearly intended to make Grenfell 'go away'. One RBKC Director in a careless moment actually admitted that it meant 'business as usual'. In protest, the Labour Group of Councillors refused to take up our positions on all Scrutiny Committees, and maintained this position for a year. The Taskforce commented:

We are disappointed that an accommodation has not yet been reached, as any uncertainty or controversy over scrutiny arrangements is a concern in the difficult circumstances that RBKC are in . . . It was premature to remove the specific Grenfell Scrutiny Committee and embed scrutiny of Grenfell Recovery in other Scrutiny Select Committees . . . We still have concerns over the pace of delivery and inconsistency in the demonstration of cultural change across the Council . . . We continue to hear community voices that tell us that they do not see sufficient change from RBKC, and they remain concerned that the Council will regress to a pre-tragedy 'business as usual' state.

In April 2020 the Labour Group reviewed their position and by majority vote rejoined the imperfect and struggling Scrutiny Committees, which had been reconvened as Select Committees. Most scrutiny by the majority Conservatives is undertaken on party lines; it is generally a battle to pursue issues of the moment and to ensure effective change. And if it is agreed to convene a Working Group or to commission a report, they are most often compromised, unhelpful and fluffy; if not, they are ignored.

What we see here in the five Independent Grenfell Recovery Taskforce reports is a Council that seems to be immune to change and committed to the status quo. A Council for whom pledges, plans and reports are a proxy for action.

It should be said that there are officers in the Council, and indeed some Councillors of all political persuasions, who worked admirably after the fire, and were patient, kind, empathic and understanding to the hundreds of affected people they met. Then there were the others, who had no natural empathy but had to attend courses on what some of us called 'Advanced Empathy and Platitudes'. You can always tell when empathy is performative; you can see it in someone's eyes. And when a senior Councillor says they are 'So so so so so sorry' in a public meeting, they stop sounding sorry and start sounding impatient.

The Charter for Bereaved Families, also known as the Hillsborough Charter, was written by Bishop James Jones in response to the treatment of families bereaved by the Hillsborough Stadium disaster in 1989. In late 2017, the Council signed up to the Charter and its six principles, which commit the Council to:

1. In the event of a public tragedy, activate its emergency plan and deploy its resources to rescue victims, to support the bereaved and to protect the vulnerable.

2. Place the public interest above our own reputation.

3. Approach forms of public scrutiny – including public inquiries and inquests – with candour, in an open, honest and transparent way, making full disclosure of relevant documents, material and facts. Our objective is to assist the search for the truth. We accept that we should learn from the findings of external scrutiny and from past mistakes.

4. Avoid seeking to defend the indefensible or to dismiss or disparage those who may have suffered where we have fallen short.

5. Ensure all members of staff treat members of the public and each other with mutual respect and with courtesy. Where we fall short, we should apologise straightforwardly and genuinely.

6. Recognise that we are accountable and open to challenge. We will ensure that processes are in place to allow the public to hold us to account for the work we do and for the way in which we do it. We do not knowingly mislead the public or the media.

The hiring of a very large and well-funded Media Communications team, encompassing community engagement, caused serious concern, and some of the team's actions – such as scant reporting on the Grenfell Inquiry – have rung loud alarm bells. The vast sum the council has spent on legal advice – up to £4.5 million a year – is a further insult to families who had to fight for the basic necessities in the aftermath of the fire, and who were expected to be grateful for the 'charity' they received.

Bishop John James' report is called 'The Patronising Disposition of Unaccountable Power'. It was, and still is, entirely apposite.

Chapter 7

THE AFTERMATH

In the aftermath of the disaster, the Council began – slowly – to look again at some of the decisions it had been making. After repeated, tireless lobbying by local campaigners, and pressure from the government to provide 'reparations' to the community after the fire, it eventually agreed to reverse the frankly appalling and undemocratic purchase of our local further education college, Wornington College. The Council had planned to demolish it and replace it with luxury homes and a non-binding commitment for a small educational space. Many people felt this was bordering on criminality.

Once this reversal had been agreed, and the Council was forced to sell the site it had bought for £26 million for a mere £10 million, it agreed to ask independent auditors to review the original purchase and the process engaged to implement it. This report – Kroll 1 – was another shocker.

The college is in the ward I have represented as Councillor since 2006, and is an integral part of many people's lives. Many local people have studied there to improve their level of education and skills and to ready them for further study or work. The college also excelled in creative arts such as fashion, theatre, pottery, music and dance. I attended flamenco classes there for eight years. Local friends who had been failed at school upgraded their skills and qualifications there on the path to becoming social workers, solicitors, teachers – and a vicar.

Despite its place as a vital resource for local people, and the very good results its excellent and committed teaching staff obtained, the college was badly run for years and was looking at financial disaster. The dark forces of the Council gathered to devour the site – and monetise it.

We local Councillors had no idea about this. Absolutely none. The Council spent £26 million of taxpayers' money with no reference to us, no consultation with stakeholders, students or staff. There was zero consultation with any Council taxpayers whatever.

The first Kroll report came out in October 2018. It was excoriating.

From a forensic investigation of letters, emails, minutes and interviews, the auditors found the following. The officer who was second in command at the Council – ironically in charge of performance, among other roles – was an external governor for the college from March 2014 to July 2017. To avoid accusations of a conflict of interest, and while engaged in a London-wide area review of further education provision, he stepped down from the Board from February to December 2016. This was the period when the deal was done, behind the backs of Councillors, staff and students.

The rules demand that: 'When a conflict of interest arises . . . (Board) members should withdraw from that part of the meeting'. Despite that, this senior officer was present at a number of meetings that discussed the potential sale to RBKC, and he 'had knowledge of the cash liquidity difficulties . . . [and was] a recipient of the February Estates Options Appraisal Assessment paper . . . which recommended the sale'. In effect, he acted as middleman, helping the college with advance payments of grants from the Council. 'Highly irregular' would be a polite assessment of his role. During this period he also met the then director of the college and attempted to broker a merger with another college. As the Kroll report stated: 'There is a concern that xx [the officer in question] helped RBKC secure the purchase of Kensington Centre [Wornington College] while [it] faced financial difficulties' and 'In February 2017, xx communicated "confidential" Ofsted reports and news about the Kensington and Chelsea College merger with City Lit to his colleagues at RBKC.' Kroll also reported on the lack of consultation: 'There is concern relating to the "secrecy" surrounding the sale of Kensington Centre. There is particularly concern regarding why RBKC did not consult or inform the local Labour Group of Councillors . . . There is concern at the lack of public consultation.' He noted that some governors were deliberately excluded from Board meetings, particularly staff and student governors, and stated that 'Such action could be perceived as a deliberate action to remove potential challenges'.

Other Board members were not entirely supine, however. A very short timeframe was being imposed, and a proposal that the sale should be agreed by 'chair's action' was put forward. One Board member demanded an explanation for why this was being proposed in 'an unholy rush . . . a fire sale'. He was 'shocked at the lack of information'.

At what point were they to begin consultation? Minutes confirm in February 2016: 'The borough have stated that they would put in place a full joint communication strategy to inform and engage the local community on their redevelopment plans', but as Kroll concluded: 'Ultimately, K&CC and RBKC did not proactively discuss the proposals, pre-sale, with the local community'. There was an 'absence of formal process' and an 'absence of adequate local community consultation': 'staff and students' governors were . . . intentionally excluded'.

In a most damning discovery, Kroll found that 'Michael Reid of law firm Pinsent Masons, which represents RBKC . . . stated on 12 May 2016: "If a rogue Councillor or third-party started making noise about RBKC doing deals in secret, etc., they would have to put out a reactive statement".'

Rogue Councillor! That's going on a T-shirt.

Following this report, further questions were asked about other property deals the Council had been involved in prior to the Grenfell Tower fire. A further audit was commissioned from Kroll, which revisited some of the findings of Kroll 1 and investigated the process behind three further deals. These were the letting of the Isaac Newton Education Centre (located in a Victorian primary school building) to Alpha Plus, a private school; the proposed letting of the North Kensington Library building to Notting Hill Prep school; and the letting of the Westway Information Centre (which housed the then Citizens Advice Bureau and some Council offices) to Notting Hill Prep, with the option for the school to let the ground floor to a coffee shop.

In all these cases, as at Wornington College, the Council did not carry out full consultation – if they carried out any at all – with local ward Councillors, let alone residents and user groups. In some cases they did not even tell stakeholders until the deals had been signed, in what was deemed to be a 'secretive bidding process'. Local

Councillors were treated with hostility by Council officers, who stated that the lack of consultation had been 'an error'. There were no options appraisals and no equality impact assessments – but there were numerous breaches of planning policy.

In relation to proposals for the College, the report states that 'The Council breached its own Local Plan', especially in relation to policy CK1: social and community use. In all cases there were changes of use in breach of our Local Plan and Supplementary Planning Documents, local strategy and planning policy. RBKC Corporate Finance stated at the time that 'The transaction does not comply with your usual financial procedure rules.'

Kroll found that Scrutiny Committee members were not provided with documentary evidence that could have helped them to raise difficult questions, and non-confidential items were put into Part B so they could not be aired publicly. At the time I asked the Town Clerk for sight of the Minutes of the secretive Property Board; I was refused.

During the lease of the Isaac Newton Centre, there had been two bids, one from Alpha Plus and the other from Notting Hill Prep, which already had a lease on a building in Lancaster Road, next to the library. There was obfuscation and confusion, with the Council apparently keen for the lease to go to Alpha Plus, and the added complication of the decision-maker, the Cabinet Member for Regeneration, etc., having his children on the waiting list for admission at both schools, while being accused of a close alliance with the owners of Alpha Plus. After an almighty row, the decision came to the committee I was then chairing, Cabinet and Corporate Services Scrutiny. We were all, cross-party, extremely concerned about this decision, which was opaque and confusing, and we were not given the documents necessary to scrutinise it in full. Then we discovered that Corporate Property had gained a 'certificate of lawful use and development' for the change of use of the property, which prevented their colleagues in Planning from assessing the potential traffic impact of the change of use. Another angle was the need to weigh up 'best value' versus 'best consideration', which pitted the highest financial value against a sum including community benefit. In a very unusual and contentious move, my committee 'called the decision in' – which meant we were called to Cabinet to question it. We were subjected to a full-on barracking from Cabinet Members, in the presence of a hundred furious parents and members of staff of Notting Hill Prep. Of course, Notting Hill Prep and Councillors supporting them lost, and Alpha Plus was successful. Clearly 'best value' had won.

North Kensington Library was built in the nineteenth century by public subscription. The plan to lease this beautiful and much-loved building to the prep school next door, to knock down the youth centre across the road and move the library into one space (including the children's library, main library and computing space on one floor, with a smaller youth centre above and two floors of private school space above that) was not welcomed by the community. Once again, the Kroll report concluded, local ward Councillors were excluded from consultation. There was no Equality Impact Assessment. Instead, an options appraisal was carried out after the decision was taken. Kroll noted that the Grenfell Action Group blog said that the Council showed 'hostility towards working-class communities'.

This leasing process took place in 2014/15. While the Isaac Newton Centre lease had been progressed, the library proposal was delayed. Community campaigners stood outside the library in the cold and rain getting signatures for their petition to save North Ken Library for public use. A campaign of misinformation by the Council which attempted to divide the community by falsely declaring that the Council was not closing the library but moving it to improved premises did not work.

After the Grenfell fire, as part of the community's demand for reparations, the Council agreed that the library would remain in its previously declared 'unfit' building and would be refurbished to its former glory: yet another gain, and a recognition of what can be achieved with community campaigning.

Sadly, the battle to save the Westway Information Centre was lost. When challenged by Kroll about a lack of consultation during the process, the Council replied that people in the area had received newsletters saying what the Council planned to happen. According to Kroll, 'the change of use [from social and community use to private school and coffee shop] can be viewed as breaching policy CK1'.

The Council used the excuse of austerity and the need to raise funds; while the Kroll report estimated that between 2010 and 2016, revenue underspends of £91.7 million were sent to capital reserves. The report also noted that equality worsened while underspends were not used, and that there was 'hostility to the concerns of the general public'. When questioned about consultation, it found that 'scrutiny occurred after decision' in these cases, and that 'income was prioritised over responsibility for communities'.

In conclusion, the Kroll report said that, while there was no evidence of criminal wrong-doing, there was wrong-doing in relation to moral and social responsibilities.

The second Kroll report came to the Audit and Transparency Committee in March 2021, a committee I then sat on. The Town Clerk attended the meeting. I questioned the repeated instances of ward Councillors being deliberately excluded from consultation, and asked how that could be seen to be reasonable as a way to avoid challenge or disagreement. Why had the Council ignored the authority of ward Councillors? The response was that, while they might ignore comments during consultation, 'Councillors add colour'. So that is all we are there for? Quite.

From the earliest days after the fire, the question of whether or not people were getting the support and financial help they needed was repeatedly asked by North Kensington Councillors and residents. In the beginning, many of the complaints was about a handful of criminals from outside the borough who had used the fire as a way of getting funds they were not eligible for, while others who were eligible found it almost impossible to get help. As MP, I had countless people coming to me – from both categories. My policy was that it was not my job to separate the sheep from the lambs. Some very credible people turned out to be thieves, and some who seemed furtive and unsure were simply traumatised and unable to communicate well. As the months went by, the Council spent vast sums of money, some wisely and some not. The question of who was overseeing this was never really answered, and as the Independent Taskforce found in their five reports, the Council worked in silos and accountability was difficult to assign.

There were also complaints that some of the volunteer groups were able to access funding for various services, while others found it difficult, if not impossible. That was simply because some people are better at filling in applications than others. It is not a fair system. Monitoring seemed non-existent. Some applicants, such as food banks, were asked to supply the Council with details of those accessing their service, which seemed a betrayal of trust as well as inequitable. Some people accessing food banks are embarrassed or ashamed about it, and it seemed very wrong to flag them up to the authorities. But, as we saw, the Director of Communities said, 'We need to separate those who need food from those who just want it.' Clearly, the director had divine judgement.

Given the constant demands for accountability, and growing accusations from the community that some groups were 'favourites' and others were unworthy of funding, we needed some clarity. As I sat on the Audit and Transparency Committee, this was my chance to demand a thorough report. It took some months but it was eventually agreed, and in May 2021 a report on Grenfell funding was published.

What I was hoping for was a warts-and-all report which, while some of it might be open to question, would at least be complete – the unvarnished truth. That was not what we were given. The report raised more questions than it answered. It was poorly laid out and included few global figures or totals. The Taskforce reports had given helpful suggestions in relation to writing reports, but sadly these didn't seem to have been taken on board by the Council and no one seemed to be monitoring progress. The report was vague and incomplete. The report stated that it provided 'the full details and breakdown of expenditure'. It didn't. The ongoing silo working, with the Grenfell Recovery Scrutiny Committee abolished before its time and Grenfell-related support spread across Council business groups, led to a financial mess, a wall of money and obfuscation, that needed to be investigated. Some of the statistics in the report were questionable. It stated that 700 people accessed services at The Curve, of which 96% were 'satisfied'. Over Covid and three lockdowns, this was frankly unbelievable. And at times, the report's tone gave the game away. Talking about the source of the £50 million recovery fund, the report stated: 'The £50 million is public money raised from Council Reserves that the Council has voluntarily committed to support recovery.'

'Voluntarily committed' is a very revealing phrase. The Council still thinks they are involved in charitable work rather than tackling an appalling situation that is of their own making.

The report tried to justify the Council's actions: 'These programmes within the Recovery Strategy were spread across the whole Council with multiple different directorates responsible and accountable for delivery . . . to ensure responsibility for Grenfell was embedded across the whole organisation to facilitate organisation-wide change and learning.' Which is waffle and nonsense.

The full picture of the financial aftermath of Grenfell is, then, that over £500 million has already been spent, £405.8 million on response and recovery, of which £105 million came from the government. A further £28 million is planned to be spent over the next three years; this doesn't include the refurbishment of Lancaster West estate, which is currently estimated to cost £57.9 million. Early estimates suggested that at the end of this very long recovery – whenever that might be – £1 billion could have been spent. The report singled out funds spent at The Curve, which was supposed to be the main place where people affected by the fire could access help. No doubt it was helpful to a lot of people, but many found it intimidating and unfriendly. The report contained no breakdown

of staffing at different levels and how much staff earned, so it provided no answers to the many questions about the alleged 'Grenfell
gravy train' for officers, which may or may not be fair. In 2022,
£500 million has been spent and there are still people from Grenfell
going hungry and being forced to access food banks. Since 2017 the
neighbourhood around the Tower has only got poorer. It is now,
for the first time, in the top six most deprived lower super-output
areas in the whole of London.

Chapter 8

CARNIVAL

Our beautiful Notting Hill Carnival started in a dark and difficult place. North Kensington had been the place of arrival for numerous West Indians (as they were then referred to) who had come over on HMS *Windrush*, or who had been demobbed in Britain after serving in the British army during the Second World War. They had been invited to stay to take on skilled and low-skilled jobs ranging from bus drivers to nurses to civil servants to factory workers. Many had a good education but had to take on low-skilled jobs, often due to institutional racism. North Kensington wasn't exactly welcoming, with its share of 'No blacks, no Irish, no dogs' signs on boarding houses, but some landlords accepted African-Caribbeans into what were often overcrowded rooms with shared, poor-quality facilities.

This was the era of Peter Rachman and the slum landlords. This era also saw a rise in anti-Black racism, and Oswald Mosley and his fascist Blackshirt supporters began to target North Ken. Mosley spoke at local venues, whipping up anti-Black racism and hatred. The race riots of 1958/9 were a sad result of these provocations.

The rise of this racism had a truly horrific consequence. In 1959 a young Antiguan, Kelso Cochrane, who was working as a carpenter during the day and studying law at night, was returning home late when he was confronted by a group of Blackshirts in Southam Street. They stabbed and killed him. It was the first murder in the UK in which racism was recorded as a motive, and it shocked the neighbourhood. There was a huge compassionate outcry. For Cochrane's funeral, which processed up to Kensal Green cemetery, thousands of local people came out onto Ladbroke Grove to show their respect, Black and white standing side by side.

From that moment, groups of residents came together. After much discussion and deliberation, they came up with a positive response to Cochrane's senseless murder – Carnival was born. The first year, it was held in a church hall. From there it grew into the huge street carnival we know today, the second largest in the world. It attracts up to one million people to North Ken over two days – and, according to the Greater London Authority (GLA), generates business worth £1 billion. In 2009 a plaque was erected where Kelso fell.

I first visited Carnival in 1980. It seemed wild and exciting. I came with a Black male friend as we had shared tastes in music and dancing; we'd both just broken up from relationships and were looking after each other. He was not my boyfriend, but as he took my hand to guide me through the crowd in All Saints Road a group of Rasta elders nodded approval, one saying, 'Now *that's* the spirit of Carnival.' I will never forget that moment.

The freedom of dancing and drinking in the street was new and exhilarating, and the atmosphere – of pure joy and love – was uplifting. But that evening as dusk fell, my friend looked panicked and shouted, 'Run this way – NOW!' As he grabbed my hand again

I peered over the peaceful dancing crowd to see a row of helmets: policemen, their arms linked, were charging at us.

Six years later I moved to North Kensington. I didn't have to go to Carnival any more; it came to me. I loved those days: the neighbourhood was transformed, with no traffic, people sitting and chatting on their front steps, everyone taking the time to talk to neighbours and strangers, the fantastic goodwill – and love – of a massive street party. The food, the music, the dancing, the costumes. You can't beat it.

Sadly, some years are blemished by criminals who come into the area to steal, sell drugs and cause trouble – which often happens at large events. Criminality disrupting Carnival is regularly used as an excuse by politicians – those who ruthlessly cut youth services and cut police funding to destroy community policing – to ban, move or drastically change it. This has led to threats to eviscerate our massive, joyful street party, with no understanding whatsoever of the importance and value to local people of the second largest cultural event on Earth. The politicians' campaign seeks to 'civilise' Carnival.

But we had five stabbings in Golborne Road one Boxing Day, and no one said we should ban Boxing Day. There was a fifty-strong riot outside Boujis nightclub in South Kensington six years ago, and they didn't close it. There was a major incident in Hyde Park when an end-of-term waterfight turned violent, and Hyde Park is still open. The list continues.

Carnival doesn't create crime. Criminals attend Carnival. Sadly, some of these criminals are very young; their lives must be desperate and hopeless indeed for them to engage publicly in such violent behaviour.

In 2015 there were two public surveys on Carnival, which set my alarm bells ringing. The Council survey was, despite local fears, a genuine attempt to review arrangements for the Carnival and run things better. To date the Council seems to 'get' Carnival – which, after all, brings a lot of money into the area. The other survey, however, from the office of my predecessor as MP, was an ill-judged effort with highly deterministic questions, which resulted in polarising opinion and inflaming tempers.

It is ironic that an event set up by local people to heal the community after Kelso Cochrane's murder is now under threat by an arguably racist and undoubtedly anti-community campaign.

Carnival is a free celebration of our wonderful North Ken melting pot in an area of London that is still shockingly, and inexcusably, poor (despite increasing gentrification). It is a wide-reaching community relations exercise whose social and community value, at a time of rising hate crime, goes far beyond its financial cost. While our communities in North Ken feel squeezed out – by estate development, rising rents, Compulsory Purchase Orders, Pay to Stay, the government's bedroom tax, rising property prices – Carnival is needed more than ever.

And there are costs. Carnival is classed as a community event, so its policing costs – £6 million each year – are not chargeable to the organisers. Ticketing would mean the policing costs would be charged, destroying the event forever. Job done for the haters.

It may sound a lot, but let's put that £6 million into perspective. The amount owed by a single embassy in Notting Hill Gate in unpaid parking fees would almost cover the cost of policing Carnival. . .

So here we are. It's one rule for them, another for us, clear as day.

We've come a long way since the police charge I saw on All Saints Road in 1980. Let's not turn back the clock.

The first year I lived on the route of Carnival, we were besieged by friends. The second year we had a small baby and ventured out to Carnival one day, rather panicked when we were caught in a crush under the Westway, whistles shrieking around us. But the baby slept on.

The artistry at Carnival in the 1980s was, to my mind, more individual and spectacular than it is today – perhaps because it was new to me. Bands came over from the Caribbean or brought Carnival designers over to help with costume-making. I interviewed one for the design magazine I was working for: hearing how these huge dramatic creations were conceived and constructed, with fabric and wire, robust enough to survive hours of dancing, possibly in wind and rain, while remaining light and comfortable enough to be worn all day, was a revelation.

In those days, there seemed to be more bands and more costumes. Some years there was a specific Carnival tune which many of the bands adopted, and sometimes a specific Carnival dance. As my children grew up, it was a point of pride to learn the song and dance moves and join in. When the whole neighbourhood was singing along to 'Who let the dogs out?' with accompanying explosions of whistles and grunts, Ladbroke Grove seemed to pound with one heart. It was uplifting.

In 2006 I was elected local Councillor – and was exposed to the flip side of Carnival. Public meetings in the run-up to Carnival with the Council, police and organisers revealed that some residents loathed Carnival's very existence. Policing what had become a huge event with up to a million visitors, I found, had many challenges.

As I've said, Carnival doesn't create crime; criminals come to Carnival. Sometimes this is to pickpocket or rob, or to sell drugs; sometimes, sadly, it's to act out territorial disputes or 'beef' in a very public arena. While this type of violent crime is usually against members of other groups and not against visitors, no one wants violent crime happening on their doorstep. It is frightening, distressing, upsetting and brings shame to the very concept of Carnival and its beginnings as a healing event and celebration in the wake of a racist murder.

All that is lost on those who see Carnival as an intrusion, an aberration, a dirty and disgusting infiltrator – and why can't the women dress decently? Some people came to public meetings to rail against the lack of toilets, the drunken behaviour, the noise and mess. Other came with clearly racist positions, and nothing could satisfy them. I am always genuinely shocked at the constant 'these people' comments I hear.

Over the years the violence has ebbed and flowed, depending on various factors. On any weekend in London, bad things happen. Compress a million people into one small area, with a few groups of people from outside the borough, determined to thieve, sell drugs or settle scores, and the numbers look bad.

After years of unfair media reporting post-Carnival, a group of us decided to fight back. We looked at the annual race meetings held at Aintree, as an example. The press always takes great delight in describing drunken women wearing short skirts and high-heeled shoes, who fall over and display their indignity and underwear. Meanwhile, some men get into drunken brawls involving broken bottles and often resulting in serious injuries.

Every year we hear threats of closure while the Carnival

community – comprising nearly everyone in North Kensington and many beyond – waits with bated breath to hear their fate: they can't help wondering if there is one set of rules for the rich and another for the poor.

Ken Livingstone was an amazing mayor in many ways, but he didn't get Carnival. After a few years of rising crime at Carnival it was proposed that Carnival be moved to Hyde Park, where a stage would be erected and people would have to pay to attend. This was a bad move on several counts. In the first place, Westminster Council, who could just about tolerate bands travelling down half a street of theirs, refused point-blank to allow it. Secondly, Carnival is not a show. You can't put it on a stage for people to watch. It's a participatory event. Without people sitting out on doorsteps or hanging out of windows, without the food stalls, without the ambience, it just isn't Carnival. It started in Notting Hill for a reason, and there it stays.

I had been an active ally of Carnival for many years: writing letters of support, refuting negative stories, going to Carnival and loving it. When I was elected MP in June 2017, it was clear that I was the first ever MP to be emphatically for Carnival, and I was asked to ceremonially open it that year.

But that year, of course, it was to take place just ten weeks after the Grenfell Tower fire. There was a lot of debate about whether or not it was appropriate to continue, or whether it would be disrespectful. We spoke to survivors, bereaved families, neighbours and other local people, and almost all of them wanted it to go ahead. It was clear that Carnival was needed now more than ever.

However, at the same time, the former MP, never a supporter of Carnival, suggested that it should be cancelled altogether, because, in her opinion, if it went ahead there would be a riot.

She was wrong.

With a lot of very sensitive community input, Carnival adapted to embrace and accommodate what had happened, with a 'quiet zone' near the Tower and a 72-second silence on both days at 3 p.m. Notices were put up to remind people to show respect, not to photograph the Tower or memorials, and to keep a respectful distance from the immediate area.

On the Sunday, a blazing hot day, I walked down to the judges' stand early. I was proud and delighted to have been invited to open Carnival. It was, quite genuinely, one of my proudest moments, and my family were there to share it. The crowd was friendly, warm and appreciative, knowing they had a true and long-time ally representing them. I said a few words, addressing in particular the children, as it was Children's Day. This is what I said:

Carnival people, when I was elected as MP to Kensington on 9 June, I was chosen for this job by 16,333 people. And that's quite a thought, because each and every single one has their own ideas of what is important and how I should serve them. I do my best every day – we are #OneKensington! But being asked to speak at the opening of Carnival is something else entirely, and it is a huge honour to be invited here to speak to you.

Young people, I live in the Carnival area. I've been coming to Carnival for many, many years and have visited mas camps. I know how much time and effort you, your families and your supporters put into these very exciting and beautiful two days. And I salute you and those who have helped you over the past weeks and months.

But I have special warmth and admiration for you young people. You are special. You have been through difficult times that most young people will never experience. I'm sure you've cried together and looked after each other. You have experienced things that have made you sensitive, brave and caring. You are the Grenfell generation, and you will grow up into sensitive, brave and caring adults, and will never forget what you learned in your childhood.

Things must change – and will change. We adults will start that process, and in years to come you will make sure that change continues. I can see some dedicated and caring future firefighters, paramedics, police, teachers, housing officers, social workers, health workers, doctors, nurses, community leaders, local Councillors – and I'm sure, out there somewhere, I can see a future Kensington MP. Nurture your ambitions!

One day soon after the fire, a friend asked me how I was. I replied, 'Just about hanging on.' Then I got a bit upset, and apologised. He was a very good friend because he said to me, 'Emma, don't. Don't ever apologise for crying, don't ever be afraid to show you're human.' And he was right. We should show that we are human and that we care for each other when we are sad or down or unhappy.

Today is a day to set aside our burden of sadness and enjoy some real joy with our families, friends and our amazing community, which the world now knows about – though it's always been here!

Carnival is for dancing, laughing, singing along and having a wonderful time with our community and those closest to us.

Today, Carnival is for you. Set aside your sadness and worries, smile, dance and sing along. And we will have the most wonderful, musical, colourful and lovable Carnival ever!

Remember, you are the Grenfell generation. You are special. Have a wonderful, blessed, safe and happy Carnival.

#RiseUpKensington!

The Mayor of London Sadiq Khan spoke after me, along with numerous faith leaders and one of our most respected community leaders, a well-known Rastafarian who called us on his horn, gave libations and blessed the event. After this we released seventy-two doves. It was a beautiful and moving ceremony, after which I walked the streets with the mayor, who was very well received.

There followed a truly peaceful and moving Carnival, with a fantastic atmosphere and far less unrest than in previous years.

And so it has been for the two subsequent years (it was then unfortunately paused by Covid in 2020 and 2021).

I have invited several parliamentary colleagues to visit Carnival with me, and each time we have thoroughly enjoyed ourselves, with little hassle even if my colleagues were recognised. By 2019 I had got to know Diane Abbott well: she had become a supporter and friend. I didn't think she would come and join me, but to my delight she did. We walked up to North Ken Fire Station to stand in silence with the firefighters – for whom as then Shadow Home Secretary she had responsibility – and they were honoured to have her there. We then walked around the northern area, picking up drinks and food as we went. The loveliest aspect of this for me was to see how relaxed Diane was and how delighted the crowds were to see her there. There was a lot of, 'Oh my God, Diane Abbott is here!' and requests for photos, which Diane seemed pleased to agree to. Having seen the frankly appalling treatment she receives daily in the media and other arenas, it was heavenly to be her lady-in-waiting for the day as she strolled around with a beatific smile on her face.

After a while we returned to my house, sat on my doorstep with a rum and coke, listened to my neighbour's sound system and drank in the atmosphere, while every so often someone yelled, 'Oh my God, Diane Abbott is on Emma's doorstep!'

It was perfect.

Chapter 9

HOGWARTS

My first days in parliament were spent in a daze. Not only had my own life changed completely and unexpectedly, but a national disaster of an unprecedented scale had occurred in my neighbourhood – now also my constituency. People were in despair, and I was supposed to set up an office in Westminster and get to grips with new procedures and protocols while not getting lost in the labyrinth of buildings, corridors, stairs and bizarrely named meeting rooms.

Since nobody had thought that Labour would win in Kensington, I was unprepared for the weird and wonderful ways of Westminster. I had visited the Houses of Parliament a few times over the years. I'd enjoyed an architecture tour to the Old Palace by a professor of neo-Gothic architecture while at uni. I'd visited with my children, and pointed out the spot in St Stephen's where their great-great-great-great-grandfather, Prime Minister Spencer Perceval, had been shot dead in 1812. I'd been to meetings held by housing campaigners when I was trying to stop the excesses of development at Wornington Green. And I had visited Harriet Harman, then Culture Secretary, to ask if she would help embarrass the Council into shutting down Opera Holland Park and to spend the £1 million a year it cost on youth services and homework clubs instead. Lobbying sometimes succeeds – but none of my efforts did.

When Harry Potter was living in a cupboard under the stairs at his auntie's, he had no idea that he was a wizard until he was bombarded with letters telling him that it was time for him to go to Hogwarts – but the Dursleys kept hiding the letters from him, and it took the intervention of Hagrid the giant to fetch him. Having lived his life with Muggles (non-wizards), Harry had a lot to learn, and his visit to Diagon Alley to buy his wand, broomstick and so on was pretty overwhelming, as was finding his way around Hogwarts.

Entering parliament as an MP for the first time isn't exactly the same as starting at Hogwarts, but there are some parallels. The neo-Gothic Old Palace, the Members' Cloakroom where you have your own peg with a loop of ribbon to hang your sword, the disappearing staircases (or so it seems when you are lost), the archaic customs, the men in tights, pudding and custard every day. I found it hard to organise getting an office, dedicated phone lines and computers. Getting passes approved for volunteers and staff took forever, meaning that for weeks on end, stuck with a visitor's pass, they had to be escorted everywhere, even to the loo. When they eventually got their pass I'd tell them, 'Go and get lost. It's the only way to find your way around this place.'

I was disappointed that there seemed to be no protocol for supporting MPs to deal with national disasters, let alone a new MP. There were no allowances made for members facing extreme circumstances. In the early days you get plenty of instructions: you are told to go to this office, sign that, don't do that, but that's just bureaucracy in relation to setting up an office. There is no manual for how to best function as an MP, and the information booklets that exist are framed in further layers of complexity. Some MPs were extraordinarily kind and helpful, and House staff were exceptional, but there seemed to be no system designed to ease new MPs into navigating the work of the House. This, while preoccupied with Grenfell and trying to do my bit to help – working with volunteers for the first eight weeks, taking distraught calls all day, visiting rescue centres regularly – was hugely challenging.

My first MP surgery was to be an open house. Around fifty people attended, and we stayed until we'd seen them all – thanks to the community centre staff, who offered to stay late. Many of my constituents were deeply traumatised – by the fire and their escape, of course – but also by the poor, disorganised treatment they had experienced after the fire. One man told us that he had come to England after being tortured in his own country, but that his treatment by the Council was 'worse than torture'. Another told me that after years of hard work they had built a life for themselves and their family and had never needed a penny from the government, 'but now they treat me like a beggar'. The Council's poor response to the disaster had taken all they had left: their dignity.

There were lighter moments, and I was hugely grateful for them. I took the 52 bus to Notting Hill Gate Station to get to Westminster. Nearly every time I got on it someone said something lovely to me – and this happened even more when I came home late. I called it 'the love bus'.

Between the election and the night of the fire, I had been bombarded with invitations. One was to a garden party in the south of my constituency, what many North Kenners would call 'the posh bit'. I had accepted enthusiastically, but after the fire I wrote to ask if they still wanted me there, as I didn't want to spoil their party with my grief and trauma. They insisted I attend. They were so welcoming and kind, it was quite overwhelming. One person said, 'We had no idea that our Council was letting down residents so badly in North Ken – the poverty it has exposed is shocking.' Several others agreed. Others complimented my campaign literature – 'You explain things properly' – which was encouraging, as I write it myself. Many enquired about my well-being. Afterward they had a 'whip-round' for Grenfell, and I was happy to direct them to a local charity with their donation: it was an incredible £10,000.

I had similar experiences at local churches and other religious establishments. I made sure I visited as many as possible: Church of England, Methodist and Catholic churches, mosques, the gurdwara and our synagogue. I had a very positive welcome wherever I went, which – so it seemed to me – went far beyond courtesy. On occasion, I forgot that what had happened at the end of my road had touched other people very deeply and shocked the world. The kindness and generosity of spirit I encountered was exceptional. Numerous people from all walks of life volunteered their time and love for Grenfell, unconditionally.

Occasionally I had survivors and the bereaved visit me in Parliament. At big meetings I was shouted at a lot, for things that weren't within my power to fix and were never mine to influence before decisions were made. That was okay; I was angry too. I took those fractious questions and demands to numerous meetings with the relevant Secretary of State and Ministers, but to no avail. I spoke to professionals at the Royal Institute of British Architects, the Royal Institute of Chartered Surveyors, the Association of British Insurers, countless MPs and several Lords, the London Fire Brigade, and unions such as the Fire Brigades Union and Unite. I met the members of the Independent Grenfell Taskforce, with whom I had far more in common in relation to issues with the Council than I could ever have imagined.

At other times, survivors and the bereaved came in individually or as a group, on a specific mission. I was very impressed and grateful that the security teams and House staff, once they'd worked out who they were, treated them so tenderly and patiently escorted them around the building. Some MPs' staff had made shameful racist comments on social media about some of my visitors, and it was heart-warming that most of the House staff, from cleaners to armed security, were unafraid to show their humanity.

Committees were another assault course. I joined the Department for Work and Pensions (DWP) Select Committee and was generously mentored by the chair, which was just as well, as there is little guidance as to how these things work. We dealt with some very difficult issues, such as the effects of benefit cuts and the implementation of universal credit on people with disabilities. Hearing their testimony, followed by the empty platitudes and defensive responses of the various organisations for imposing these tortuous new systems, was infuriating. I was on the committee for a year, and believe that Select Committees do some of the most effective work in parliament.

Over time I joined some All Party Parliamentary Groups (APPGs), the most relevant being the Fire Safety and Rescue APPG, whose chair was the late David Amess MP. David was thorough, hard-working, caring, very supportive and kind. How anyone could target him as the recipient of hate is incomprehensible. The APPG had been doing sterling work for many years, and it emerged in the Grenfell Inquiry that the Group had written thirteen times to the government after the Lakanal House fire in 2009, asking them to implement the recommendations of the coroner at the Lakanal House Inquest. If the government in power – Labour until 2010, Coalition and Tory since then – had acted on this, the flammable materials responsible would not have been used on high-rise buildings and seventy-two lives would have been saved at Grenfell.

It was tempting to join numerous APPGs of interest; actually finding the time to attend them, let alone be effective in them, was something else entirely. Some are funded by the very organisations who wish to control the issue being investigated. They literally set up an APPG with an amenable MP to steer investigations away from problems they have identified. Not mentioning any names . . .

Another committee I joined was the cross-house, cross-party group, the Joint Committee on the Draft Registration of Overseas Entities Bill, which sounds tedious in the extreme but was fascinating. The group was working on legislation that would force the anonymous overseas owners of valuable property – the 'beneficial owners' – to disclose who they were. No more shell companies hiding the owners of empty flats! Of course they wanted the MP for Kensington to be involved, as we had so many empty homes in the borough while thousands of residents were homeless.

I found that there were some thoroughly unpleasant people in Westminster. A culture of misogyny and sexism brought me back to the 1970s, temping in offices in my holidays from college, when dirty comments, touching and innuendo were commonplace. Despite decades working in the male-dominated worlds of journalism in design and architecture, I hadn't encountered this kind of behaviour for years. Work colleagues were work colleagues. If anything else occurred it was private, out of the workplace. I certainly didn't expect, during a tour of the Lords, to have my thigh stroked by a possibly drunk peer. Daytime drinking in parliament is common, and while there are certainly occasions when it may be appropriate to celebrate before sundown, it's shocking to see staff and MPs drunk during the day. I can deal with being sneered at, but being slobbered over by an out-of-control drunk, in the lobby while waiting to vote on matters of state, is just shocking. After a series of incidents, the staff bar was closed for a period then re-opened, in the evenings only, under a different name. It was still a hotbed of intrigue and I certainly didn't expect my staff to spend much time there.

The House of Commons terrace, which overlooks the Thames and is an iconic spot, can be lovely on a warm evening. I often took my staff there for an end-of-day wind-down before heading home. It could be collegiate and friendly – but we were warned to watch our backs there, as gossip abounds and you never know who may be standing right beside you, listening in! There is also some unseemly conduct. One night I watched as a young woman, surrounded by fawning older men, was plied with drink until she could hardly stand. I waited until she went to the loo and followed her, meaning to escort her into a taxi. But, sensibly, she had disappeared.

A lot of men working in Parliament need to remember what they're there for, and behave better.

Aside from feeling that I had time-travelled back to the 1970s, it was an extraordinary thirty months. Doing my utmost to always put the needs of my constituents first, tackling quite devastating issues through casework for Grenfell-affected residents, trying to push forward on legislation that would improve life for my

64,000 constituents and improve building safety and fire safety was a juggling act for which my best could never really be enough. Interestingly – and flatteringly – I was told over and again that I was the best constituency MP that Kensington had ever had, and that it was heart-warming for residents to see that I cared about them all – which I did, and still do. Since I lost my seat in December 2019 I've been asked over and again by people all across the constituency if I would stand for parliament again. My response is always, 'Would you vote for me if I did?'

Everyone who has asked me that question said they will indeed vote for me again. So perhaps I will. . .

Chapter 10

CONSEQUENCES AND REPERCUSSIONS

Having covered the Council's ambitious programme of development, gentrification or regeneration – call it what you will – it is now sensible to review the outcome of all this work. When in 2013 the Audit and Transparency Committee questioned the capacity of the Council to deliver this humungous programme of change through development, the committee was reassured by the Director of Property's words: 'There are first-class checks and balances in place. The team is in full control.'

So let's do some checks. With so many project timetables overlapping, it is impossible to review them in chronological order, so instead they are considered geographically, starting in the south of the borough, covering the period 2012–2017 (with some later insights, as at early 2022).

A planning application for a development on part of the Cremorne Wharf site on the Thames at Lots Road went to the Planning Committee in 2012. The stated intention was to 'safeguard the value of the site' before it was leased long-term to Thames Tideway for the Tideway Tunnel flood prevention works. In other words, the Council wished to inflate the value of the site. The lease of the site for Tideway works was due to complete at the end of 2021; whether or not previous plans for residential development on part of this site will actually happen remains to be seen. Project: stalled, but we're watching.

Proposals for a Crossrail 2 station on King's Road were put forward in 2014. There were two potential sites for this: one at the junction of Sidney Street and King's Road; the other on Cremorne estate next to World's End. The Council was fully behind this plan, their priority being the potential bulldozing of Cremorne estate along with the full development of this precious King's Road location, including a huge shopping mall. After an extensive local campaign involving residents from all walks of life – and a bad-tempered public meeting at Chelsea Old Town Hall in 2015 – Transport for London withdrew the proposal. Project: stopped by local activism.

Hortensia Road, Chelsea, with the Kensington and Chelsea College buildings and the listed Carlyle Building, was the subject of a great deal of controversy. A site on Fulham Road was developed for luxury flats, as was the Carlyle Building. The college's car park, after a huge row among Tory Councillors about its use class (provoking the comment from a senior Councillor, 'If this proposal came from a developer, we'd have his guts for garters'), was built by Grainger into a mixed tenure development, including homes for private rent. After the Grenfell Tower fire the Council bought the development back to use as homes for households made homeless by the fire. There were endless snagging problems with this development, which eventually proved not to be fire-safe. Project: completed but to very poor construction standards.

Denyer Street depot and its neighbour Marlborough School were targeted for extensive redevelopment, involving replacing the primary school on a smaller, but much taller, site, and adding private residential homes for rent. Again there was a huge local campaign against this, with attempts to have the Victorian school building listed. These sadly failed. Project: achieved by RBKC.

The large square at Elm Park Gardens, with its communal gardens, had derelict basement units that were, with some persuasion from the government and me, put back into use: there was a mix of unconverted shell properties sold on the open market (local estate agents told me that the Council undersold them), and some homes were converted to social rent and keyworker homes. Project: achieved by RBKC.

When developer CapCo bought the Earls Court Exhibition Centre site and brought forward plans to demolish it and develop it into a new 'urban village', RBKC supported it wholeheartedly. The loss of the world-renowned music venue and exhibition space in 2014, which the Greater London Authority stated brought business worth an annual £1 billion into London, was considered acceptable. Eight years later the site has been bulldozed and resold. It remains empty, despite plans from another developer owner being initiated. Meanwhile the hotels, restaurants, cafes and shops that relied on exhibition centre trade have suffered, and many have closed. Project: stalled (for ten years to date from decision).

The hidden-away Council estate of Chesterton Square and Broadwood Terrace, built on top of Council offices on the corner of Warwick Road and Pembroke Road, was targeted in 2014/15 for development. This very successful small estate had numerous leaseholders, who were approached to be bought out at market rate plus a premium. Some, afraid of losing the value of their homes, sold out early. Some of their homes were then let out by the Council as temporary accommodation, charging the government full market rate, while others were let out privately. Some lease-holders stayed and protested strongly to save their estate. Project: stopped (post-Grenfell), now to be refurbished.

The Council-owned car park in Young Street, just off Kensington High Street, also housed the parking offices and a law firm (which the Council denied was there, in order to achieve change of use). In 2013/14 this was developed by the Council, with Grainger as the developer partner, into luxury private housing. Project: achieved by RBKC.

The full demolition and development of Holland Park School included selling off the southern playground for super-prime housing development, as described in chapter one. The school project was plagued with problems due to poor construction stand-ards, a leaking swimming pool, self-opening windows that opened and shut too often, disturbing pupils, and poorly attached cladding panels that fell off. It has been controversial since the start. Even though the new school opened in 2012, there were so many ongoing snags that the Council has only leased the school short-term, and in 2022 was still financially liable for ongoing defects. The playground development, Campden Villas, was still partially unsold after nine years. Project: completed, to poor construction standards. Poorly scrutinised by Trustees, most of whom resigned in 2021.

As part of the Council's plan to 'improve' the environment neigh-bouring the Westway flyover, there were five concurrent projects involving Council buildings. All of these were highly contentious and attracted huge public protests. The Isaac Newton Professional

Development Centre, used for training teachers, among other educational services, was the subject of criticism in the second Kroll report ('the Council breached its own policies'). It was eventually leased to an exclusive primary school. Project: achieved by RBKC.

The Council building at Malton Road, behind Ladbroke Grove Station, had been used as a day centre and lunch club for elders, specialising in people with dementia. A plan to close this service down and replace it with Council offices was pushed through. However, the build quality was so poor that the offices had to be closed for three months so the contractor could repair the leaking roof (under the Westway), continually flooding toilets, and rat infestation; the drains had not been fitted with valves to stop backflow. Project: completed, to poor construction standards.

A further embedding of private schools in the area involved three buildings: North Kensington Library, Lancaster Road Youth Club and the Westway Information Centre (WIC), which had originally been leased to Citizens Advice Bureau. How the conversion of these three essential local public services to private use was ever considered politically justifiable is mystifying. The WIC underwent a rapid, but controversial, change of use class and was refurbished with a private nursery above and a café at street level. The library and youth club, however, after a fierce battle by local campaigners, was saved post-Grenfell as part of reparations to the community. Projects: WIC – completed. Library – saved in perpetuity. Youth club – saved for now.

The Council is the landlord of the 23 acres immediately underneath the Westway. This land was leased to the Westway Trust for use by the community as compensation for the flyover that cut the area in two, destroying several streets. Given the gradual gentrification of the area, it became an area of interest to property developers, and one such was appointed to lead the Westway Trust. Proposals for the area under the Westway, from Acklam Road in the eastern part of K&C to the stables in the western part, began to emerge. All the charities and voluntary organisations that were housed beneath the Westway came under scrutiny, and one by one were threatened with closure. The Westway Trust said it needed more income to survive, but given the £10 million it had in reserves at the time, this was nonsense. A master plan for 'Destination Westway' was put out to consultation; it included designer shops and an exclusive restaurant on stilts overlooking Portobello Green. Local people could see that these were not for their benefit, but for newcomers. Visitors came to shop on Fridays and Saturdays. All the visuals featured white hipsters. Who would use these new high-end shops and restaurants the other five days of the week? At one consultation event, the chair of a residents' association asked the Cabinet Member what local people on low incomes were supposed to do with shops selling £1,000 handbags. 'Earn more money and buy handbags!' was the disgraceful response. The plans went to committee. After well-argued objections by local representatives, the project was deferred. By 2021 the Westway Trust had been taken over by local activists, long-term plans were being revisited, and 'Destination Westway' had been shelved entirely. Project: stopped by local activism.

Alongside these ambitious plans for monetising Council 'assets' were some terrifying plans for Council estates in North Kensington. While we needed an additional secondary school, we did not want it to take up valuable amenity space at the foot of Grenfell Tower. Despite protests, it was built on this site. The school build apparently went well, is fire-safe and insulated with mineral wool, and well designed. The rebuilt Kensington Leisure Centre, however, is fraught with problems. The roof leaked from day one, the hot water and shower facilities were constantly problematic, and there were numerous other problems. School: completed to good construction standards. Leisure centre project: completed but badly.

The former front car park of the leisure centre was earmarked for development to private rented homes. While the project was slowed due to the Grenfell Tower fire, it was finally completed. The Council then negotiated with the development partner Grainger to retain the new housing for Grenfell homeless families. Project: completed then bought back.

Middle Row School was also earmarked for development, with residential units to be built on the playground and to replace the school-keeper's house. Another Grainger build, and the homes had countless snags, necessitating digging up floors to relay drains. Project: completed, with some issues.

A row of working garages off Portobello Road was part of this group of developments. The local mechanics were evicted with little notice, even those who had been in business there for forty years. After a ten-year delay, a row of houses was built there. These also had snagging issues and could not be occupied for two years. Project: completed, badly.

The most devastating plans that would affect the largest number of tenants and leaseholders were the Council's proposals for Silchester West, the estate opposite Latimer Road Station that was bookended between the railway and the Westway. Despite its unpromising location, it was very well designed, with low blocks running around a large landscaped communal garden, four twenty-storey blocks and some two-storey houses. All in all, it was a success story for the 1960s Council, which had demolished genuine slums to build the estate, and for the residents, who were very close-knit. A concerted campaign against the demolition and development of the estate seemed to be going nowhere until the shoddily refurbished Grenfell Tower met its horrific fate and brought this monstrous plan to an end. Project: stopped post-Grenfell, to be refurbished.

A further round of proposals focused on four projects: small housing blocks in Raddington Road and Oxford Gardens (both giving on to Portobello Road, so clearly too valuable for social tenants), a row of two-storey homes in Portland Road, and a mews of small one-bed homes off Ladbroke Grove. Four projects: all stopped post-Grenfell.

Another estate destined for bulldozing was Balfour Burleigh towards the north of Ladbroke Grove, a large estate with communal gardens and games space. It had two rather well-designed twenty-storey towers and was otherwise low-rise, with some front and back gardens, clearly well-loved and well cared for. The Council's plan to develop this into what a Cabinet Member called the 'future South Kensington' was devastating for many tenants, who had lived there for decades. The development was to include the primary school, Barlby School: its playground was to be built over for residential homes and a separate unit for children with special needs. In the event, the school and playground were developed but the estate was saved. It was at this school in spring 2021 that local residents found piles of flammable insulation by Kingspan, the company that had supplied Grenfell Tower. This was removed after protest. Project on Barlby School: achieved. Project on Balfour Burleigh estate: stopped post-Grenfell.

While there were, and are, many smaller developments in the running and heading for 'trickle transfer' to semi-private or fully private use, these were the major schemes that aroused the most public dissent. The final project, Wornington College, our further education facility which, as we saw earlier, was purchased by the Council for development into private flats, was not only stopped by determined, relentless community activity, but post-Grenfell it was completely turned around: the Council was forced by the government to resell the building to be used as a college in perpetuity. The Council was made to sell it at a loss of £15 million – a total humiliation that it somehow spun into a 'gain' of £10 million and a victory for local education. Project: stopped by determined local activism.

The ongoing fantasy of Kensal Gasworks Crossrail station, or 'Portobello Crossrail' as the Council called it, is totally shameful. Back in the noughties, it may have been possible to locate a Crossrail station at the gasworks, but the Council hesitated and missed the moment. Since then it has maintained the myth that Crossrail, under the auspices of Transport for London, was about to make a final decision on the potential station, and how very exciting it was. We were literally told to expect a decision 'in about two weeks' so many times that it became a joke. Meanwhile the Council spent millions of pounds of taxpayers' money on feasibility studies for a project that everyone knew – apart from local developers and their clients – would come to nothing. Project: stopped, at vast expense (as yet unquantified) to Council taxpayers. But the promise of the Crossrail station boosted the value of nearby developments.

The Tri-borough project, conceived to 'save money by combining services', was, in the words of a senior Tory Councillor, 'an unmitigated and entirely predictable disaster'. On one contract alone, £10 million was wasted. I have been unable to find out how many tens of millions were spent altogether. If the then Leader of the Council was pinning his hopes of a peerage on its success, he had to make do with a mere knighthood. Project: stopped, at vast expense.

Since the Council increases its assets by buying homes for temporary accommodation outside the borough, thereby making a profit by pocketing the difference between the cost of maintaining the properties and the value of housing benefit paid by government, we should account for this appropriately. Residents' lives are being destroyed by a Council that refuses to build sufficient social rented homes on its own land but instead moves them out of borough, building up its own property portfolio and profiting from government benefits. Project: achieved (sadly).

So where does all this leave us? There is some good news among all the gloom and doom: namely, that of the thirty-five projects discussed above, nineteen were stopped – slightly more than half. There are numerous reasons for this, but many were stopped by community activism and campaigning by people who refused to take 'yes' for an answer.

Please note that when the Council insists that it can only afford to develop estates if it doubles the number of homes on them, the 'net additional' homes are sold or let on the private market. This obviously attracts incomers, who often rent them out or use them for short lets via Airbnb. So in effect, social tenants contribute to a system where the rent they pay enables leaseholders or private renters from outside the borough to profit from the homes subsidised by social tenants.

One example was the proposals for Silchester West, which was supposed to replace 'like for like' the number of social rented homes when it was developed. The so-called 'right to return' after a development process that could take five years was at first a guarantee, then became conditional, 'where possible'. Given the degree of overcrowding that is rife across North Kensington, it would never be possible to guarantee a right to return unless there was a genuine increase in the number of homes available for social rent. Frankly, the Council depends on many households not returning after development.

Those who did return at Wornington Green found that their rent had increased, the service charge had increased, and they were in a much higher council tax band, even if they had the same number of bedrooms as they did previously. They hadn't been told any of this before development. They had been told they would be charged 'at the same rate', which is not the same as 'the same cost'. Often the new flats have a larger floor area due to being designed to Lifetime Homes standard – a well-intentioned policy that incorrectly presumes that every single person will in later life graduate to using a wheelchair, which is clearly not the case.

Many people with limited physical ability do not like to be placed on upper floors, making the implementation of the Lifetime Homes standard redundant. Lifts break down, and people are then stuck. This concern was common before the Grenfell Tower fire, where lifts regularly broke down, and the fire rescue override malfunctioned on the night of the fire. Since the fire, very few people with limited physical ability – or indeed with young children – have been happy to be placed on higher floors.

So how would the Council judge its own success over the past ten years, in financial terms? And who should hold the Council to account for its failures? Should we sit by and watch the Council mark its own homework?

We can start by looking at the rules, regulations and statutory duties that the Council has to abide by, according to law. There are numerous laws governing all this, and it's difficult to unpick them all; they often seem to overlap or to conflict and contradict. Here, though, are the basic needs that do seem to be solidly enshrined in law, as stated in the Human Rights Act 1998, Article 8: Respect for your private and family life:

1. Everyone has the right to respect for his private and family life, his home and his correspondence.
2. There shall be no interference by a public authority with the exercise of this right except such as is in accordance with the law. . .

That ought to be that: in fact, a whole slew of other laws – the national planning policy, various Housing Acts, the Department for Communities and Local Government's Statutory Duties – also apply in this area, and only serve to make the issue more complicated. But we can see from the Human Rights Act 1998 what the aim ought to be.

We have also already seen that the Council has some fantastic policies: the problem is that the Council does not implement them. As I was told by a qualified outsider: 'RBKC write policy as a proxy for action.' One of these policies is the heart-warming 'Towards an Inclusive Kensington and Chelsea', which covered the period 2007–10. Its objective was to 'improve the life chances of people living in the most deprived communities in the borough' by 'preventing ill health and disability' and to 'reduce the gap in average life expectancy between the north and south of the borough'. As we have seen in earlier chapters, sadly the reverse occurred: in our beautiful borough, life expectancy has increased in wealthier areas and decreased, quite shamefully, by six years over a ten-year period in poorer areas. According to the updated Marmot Report of February 2020, this is the worst decrease in the entire country.

Since the Grenfell Tower fire, with the world watching, our failing Council has produced some truly magnificent reports, reviews and policies, many of which I have quoted from already. One was a self-declared and self-important 'Green Paper' by the new Deputy Leader, who was put in charge of Housing and Regeneration as well as Grenfell Recovery. 'Kensington and Chelsea Homes: Solving the challenge together' seemed well-meaning but was ultimately ineffective, packed with, as one resident put it, 'statements of the bleeding obvious'. One phrase that came back to haunt the Deputy Leader was, 'We genuinely put residents at the heart of our housing decisions', along with a regularly repeated commitment to 'co-design', without, however, an explanation of what this would look like to RBKC. The paper committed to use local small to medium-sized enterprises, to pay a living wage (not the London Living Wage, of course), and to involve residents in the recruitment of housing management staff. This last was somewhat redundant as some ill-tempered and poorly trained KCTMO staff were TUPEd over to the Council – which means their contracts were transferred with precisely the same pay and conditions, but with no oversight or redress for tenants. The Green Paper proposed a full stock survey (we're still waiting for this after four years) and annual visits to tackle illegal subletting. There was a commitment to 'keep residents in the home', especially where rent or council tax arrears were an issue. The Council would use debt counsellors, not bailiffs. Much of this aspirational fluff was not implemented.

After admitting in July 2017 that an early mistake the Council made after the fire was to think 'we could do this on our own', the Council did not appoint suitably experienced and skilled officers to advise on their work – or if they did, they refused to take their proposals on board. There was no acknowledgement of ongoing failures; instead they battened down the hatches and released endless 'good news' stories via their £1 million a year comms team.

The Deputy Leader's paper again anticipated that Kensal Gasworks was a 'potential location for Crossrail', even though we had been told numerous times, including by the chair of Crossrail himself, that this would never happen. And the Deputy Leader made this commitment in relation to Kensal Gasworks: 'We will be starting real community engagement on this site later this year and will use this process to show how the Council has changed.' Which indeed it did, as the proposals for this site repeated the myth about the fantasy Crossrail station, and supported the usual demeaning 'gazebos in car parks' consultation exercises.

The paper expressed general disapproval of housing associations selling off properties to invest in cheaper areas – despite the Council continuing to do this itself! We were informed that the Council was lobbying the Ministry of Housing, Communities and Local Government to extend Empty Dwelling Management Orders – by which a local authority can take over long-term empty properties and let them – to apply to all empty properties, not just (as currently) to dilapidated buildings. But nothing came of that either.

There was great excitement about the New Homes Programme, a plan for 300 new social rented homes to be built in the borough using funds from the Mayor of London. Despite the £100,000 that was awarded per home, the scheme had to be 'self-financing', which meant building a further 300 homes for private sale or rent. This, as we know, was to be built on land the Council told us repeatedly it did not have. The new development was to be 'of the highest standard' and progressed via an 'Open Book Zone', whereby anybody could scrutinise the financial status of these projects.

It all sounded very exciting, but little of all this bore fruit.

The Deputy Leader's opening statement in his 'Green Paper' was: 'The Grenfell tragedy has changed Kensington and Chelsea forever. There can be no going back to the old ways of working. . . . I am in a unique position to advocate for change.' His final words were: 'We actively seek your views' – which is one way of saying 'tell us what you want and we'll continue to ignore it'.

As the Grenfell Taskforce reports identified further areas of weakness and errors in the work of the Council, the Council published a number of wide-ranging community engagement papers and surveys throughout 2018 and 2019. 'Creating Stronger Communities' was very much a part of the wider Grenfell recovery, which was to be 'community led'. Out of an estimated 11,000 people who had been affected by Grenfell, the team spoke to 300 at physical meetings. About 600 people looked at the online consultation. However, only sixteen – SIXTEEN PEOPLE! – engaged with it, a clear demonstration of residents' lack of belief in the process bringing any genuine improvement.

Having been criticised by the Grenfell Taskforce for the ineffectiveness of its scrutiny under the Scrutiny Committee system, the Council proposed a whole new way of working via Select Committees. I had worked in Parliament under the Select Committee system, and the Council's version was nothing like the original. The number of meetings was to be reduced, the number of committees was to be reduced, and oversight of decisions was left to a single committee, the Overview and Scrutiny Select Committee. The worst aspect of this proposal was that it eliminated the Grenfell Recovery Scrutiny Committee entirely, moving responsibility for this instead into the relevant Select Committees. The Labour Group – and North Ken residents – saw this for what it was: a determined, inappropriate and untimely proposal to shut residents out of the decision-making process altogether and eliminate the anger and upset that the members and attendees of the Grenfell Recovery Scrutiny Committee had felt – an anger that arose because of the Council's poor decision-making and lack of progress and care. The proposals were discussed by the Labour Group of Councillors, and we decided to step out of scrutiny altogether in protest – as I have mentioned before – but we watched and questioned the Council nonetheless. We stuck to this for a year, from May 2019 to May 2020, when, with the pandemic raging, we returned to take up our places on Council committees.

After over a year of supposed consultation, the Council came up with yet more policies and strategies. The 'People Strategy' of December 2019 – which was, well, a bit thin – set out 'Our Vision': 'We will embed new values and behaviours for our workforce, the people that are here to serve our communities and provide the services they need.' Given that the Council continued to receive complaints from the public about the 'behaviours' of some members of the RBKC workforce, I can't comment on how the 'four key pillars' of 'Putting Communities First', 'Respect', 'Integrity' and 'Working Together' have served residents at all. Six pages of mostly stock photos are simply inadequate for the task of any 'People Strategy'.

The 'Youth Review' was yet another ambitious project doomed to fail, as youth services were due to be cut by £1 million. Mentions of 'co-design' in this context are meaningless. Numerous ideas, some very good, were aired through this process, but some of the key issues the Council should have dealt with – such as mental health, careers guidance, academic support, raising awareness among young people of the services available to them, and particularly the development of safe parks and open spaces – were clearly left on a shelf somewhere gathering dust, along with the majority of these 'initiatives'.

I have sat on committees for more than ten years periodically discussing procurement via local businesses; nothing has really changed and it seems unlikely to change after the 'Social Value Strategy' has been considered. The Council's procurement system still needs an overhaul; the Procurement Scrutiny Working Group's report, finally published in late 2016 with 182 recommendations, made little difference to how the Council procures or to improving accountability by using local businesses to deliver services. The benefits of working with your local community are well known. No one loses. But it takes a genuine and wholehearted commitment to do this – and, as we know, the Council lacks that. The Public Services (Social Value) Act 2012 is 'an Act to require public authorities to have regard to economic, social and environmental well-being in connection with public services contracts'. This is a statutory requirement, yet monitoring of this is often haphazard. Of course it's a positive that the

Council has committed to pay staff and contracted staff the London Living Wage, which Labour Councillors have been demanding for nearly ten years. As ever, numerous commitments and 'challenges' have been laid out throughout these policies, but I want to mention here how the Council dealt with climate change. Along with declaring a climate emergency, the Council make token gestures such as providing plug-in electricity charging points in lampposts for those who own electric cars, while refusing to provide a safe cycling network for residents. Here we see, once again, ambition overreaching what can be achieved within the current ideological framework.

The Council's Charter for Public Participation was another ambitious attempt to draw thousands of disaffected residents into decision-making, to 'help shape the decisions made by the Council and to contribute to the development of services, plans and programmes alongside Council officers and local Councillors'. Most of it is aspirational nonsense that residents know will be ignored. The Charter stated that residents must be 'given an opportunity to be involved in advance' of major proposals, and 'where there is clear local consensus, [this should be] taken into account in Council decisions' to 'co-design or co-produce and . . . facilitate that involvement where possible'. It is never possible. Residents' campaigns and demands continue to be ignored, despite the Council's commitment to 'continue to review the way that we have engaged with local people and consider how we might improve'. Along with a commitment to 'keep ward Councillors informed of issues and developments that have a particular impact on their wards and alert them well in advance to decisions that have a significant impact on their constituents', the Charter had huge ambitions but no route map to achieve them. Despite this, the Council assures us that 'the Charter is not purely aspirations but, rather, is the catalyst for and reflection of real culture change' – a culture change that is as fantastical as the Portobello Crossrail station.

Much hope has been invested in the Council Plan 2019/23, which once again has more stock photos and pastel-coloured graphs than actual content: twenty-one pages of filler out of a total of thirty-five. Without embarrassment the Plan repeats the Hillsborough Charter that the Council signed up to after the fire, which commits to: 'place the public interest above our own reputation'; 'approach . . . scrutiny . . . with candour, in an open, honest and transparent way . . .'; 'avoid seeking to defend the indefensible or to dismiss or disparage those who may have suffered where we have fallen short'; and 'ensure all members of staff treat members of the public and each other with mutual respect and with courtesy. Where we fall short, we should apologise straightforwardly and genuinely.' Other commitments made include: 'listen to what local residents want and be guided by their views on any changes to neighbourhoods'; 'make it easy for people to complain and take effective enforcement action to get licensing, planning and traffic management rules obeyed'; 'tackle the development of new flats that are built only to be left empty'; and 'co-create a new youth offer with local children and young people'. Given the Council's current plans to cut a further £1 million from youth services, this is simply dishonest.

A final comment is equally bemusing: 'Ultimately we aspire to rebuilding trust with our communities and reconnecting with our residents by being open, transparent and engaging, and putting local people at the heart of the decision-making process.'

For anyone who has been involved in the Council's post-fire 'engagement', this will provoke a hollow laugh.

The irony of the Council romping through a catalogue of poorly managed developments with their 'partners', then having to buy them back to rehouse homeless families from Grenfell, then having to repair the countless faults they were responsible for, is surely a metaphor for the Council which sells its borough as the 'best place to visit, live and work'.

The Council does not like to be held to account by recognised outside individuals or bodies. It uses its expensive comms team and every trick in the book to minimise, reframe, question, undermine or even defame those who do. At one point I wondered what they thought of me, and especially what the internal discussions were within the Council when, as MP, I continually questioned and criticised the Council. I am entitled to this information. In April 2019 I put in a Subject Access Request. I got no response whatever. Two months later I re-sent it, citing my earlier request, which the Council insisted it had not received. Then I was told it would be too costly to provide the information I had requested, as it covered 131,000 emails. I halved the time period I had requested, but was informed that it would still be too costly as 65,000 emails included my name. I persisted, asking for shorter and shorter time periods until it was three months, then just one month after my election.

Finally, in January 2020, nine months after my initial request, I received their response. It comprised twelve pages of emails. Every single word was blacked out, apart from one paragraph written by the former Town Clerk on the day after my election in 2017. It said, over and over in the otherwise blacked-out email trail, 'I did then return to the colours [a technical term meaning the count administration] at 5 p.m. so that Tony [second in command at the Council] could say that colleagues had monitored the recount from every angle. It was quite extraordinary to watch Cllr Dent Coad give her short and sweet victory speech (including thanking the Liberal Democrat for taking votes away from Lady Borwick!).' For a senior public servant, this was a pretty shocking comment. I had to wonder what was behind the many blacked-out paragraphs.

The bad news kept on coming. Our failing Council was under constant review from various outside bodies, such as the Centre for Governance and Scrutiny (CfGS). These reviews are an ongoing cat-and-mouse game for a Council that is fiercely protective of its practices and thereby ill-prepared for genuine change. The Council is prone to sitting on critical reports for a month or two until it has prepared a positive spin on one seemingly neutral comment. The Council does not learn. Instead, when a problem emerges, it is drowned out with meaningless activity rather than a meaningful solution. Or the Council runs a spate of 'training' activities and writes yet more 'reviews' that do nothing to change how the Council actually functions, but instead puts a positive spin on the ongoing chaos.

In July 2021 a 'Scrutiny Stocktake' exercise took place under the auspices of the CfGS. This reviewed the changes to scrutiny – referred to a the 'New Model of Scrutiny' that the Council had implemented in 2019, despite serious concerns raised by the Labour Group of Councillors and of course from the Independent Grenfell Recovery Taskforce that had specifically advised against some of the changes, especially the abolition of the Grenfell Recovery Scrutiny Committee. The so-called 'detailed action plan' the CfGS drew up after the stocktake included the following: 'In some areas members have not got a grip on how to maintain a "watching brief" on critical service matters'; 'Scrutiny does not focus systematically on the change process and its engagement with corporate risk . . . [and] . . . is quite superficial.' The CfGS also noted a 'lack of consistent systems to monitor the executive's implementation of recommendations that have been accepted' and that 'minuting practice can make it difficult to determine where and when recommendations have been made . . . lack of general insight on scrutiny's outcomes'. Most gratifyingly: 'Since Labour's re-engagement, the overall quality and effectiveness of scrutiny has improved. This goes hand in hand with more effective chairing.' The report continued:

> There have been occasions where Lead Members and senior officers have sought to influence the work programme of individual committees. . . . It does harm perceptions of the function's independence and raises risks around scrutiny's ability to engage in robust and challenging work. It also reflects the continuation . . . of the 'fuzziness' of roles which we described in 'Change at the Council'.

The review of Grenfell scrutiny echoed much of what we all feared when the 'improved system' was introduced in 2019:

> The local community, and many Councillors, have rightly asserted the need for rigorous oversight of operational matters relating to the area and support for those affected by the tragedy. [. . .] This operational oversight and scrutiny must be carried out in a way that commands the confidence of local people.

An Interim Review of Governance by CfGS went to committee in October 2021. This had been delayed for a year due to Covid, as had the Scrutiny Stocktake. Once again, there was plenty for the Council to take on board. There was criticism of the obscurity of 'process and systems used to develop decisions' and a recommendation that decision-making should be clearly mapped so that outsiders could follow the process. A 'longer-term approach' was suggested for policy development, which some people took to be a clear criticism of short-sighted and aspirational policy documents that led to nothing. There was criticism about one of the issues that had been identified in the Procurement Scrutiny Working Group Report undertaken in 2016, relating to work needed on contracts before tendering. There was a polite reminder that Council members and officers should be made familiar with the Charter for Public Participation, echoing our own concerns about a lack of cultural change. And the suggestion that officers should take training to better understand the role of elected members reflected the concern of so many people that senior officers in particular see themselves as the executive, and Councillors (particularly minority party Councillors) as working for them.

The findings of the Report encouraged the Council to embrace 'the aim of the Council "living" the Charter's principles. This includes publicising their understanding about what "consultation" is, and how and when the expectation might be present that the Council will consult'.

My concerns were summed up in this verdict: 'We were told by a number of people that they felt that the Council uses the act of strategising, and of reviewing and evaluating strategic changes it has made, as a proxy for taking meaningful action.'

Other comments relating to 'a more candid approach to engagement and decision-making' certainly reflected the concerns of many residents who continue to feel the Council continues to obfuscate and clothe decision-making in opaque procedures. All in all, this was yet another critical review of the Council's post-Grenfell failure to progress.

Chapter 11

COMPASSIONATE KENSINGTON

In November 2021 a hard-fought-over vestige of the Kensington Odeon cinema in Kensington High Street was demolished, as it was said to be 'unstable'. The beautiful facade was the only part that had been retained after planning permission for demolition and development was granted, and it had been held up by scaffolding for six years as the building work had stalled.

Architectural heritage specialists and campaign groups fought to save the unique Art Deco building, which – despite later additions – had retained its beautiful lobby with double marble staircases. Behind modern panelling some original interior detailing was uncovered that had been thought to be lost.

Titans of the film industry recalled the numerous world pre-mieres that had been held there, including Alfred Hitchcock films, and all the film stars who had walked the red carpet over the hundred years the cinema had been open. Current film directors and actors wrote to plead with the developer to preserve its history, restore the theatre and improve facilities in the building around it – with additions, if they must. Residents and residents' associations attended packed planning meetings, debating every point, until the dreaded permission was granted. I remember one young woman who attended a meeting dressed as a tree. She wanted to save the two magnificent plane trees in front of the cinema. She cried inconsolably when permission was granted for demolition, though the trees were saved in a later iteration.

As so often happens, it is during a campaign such as this that local people, whose only communications with the Council relate to clean streets, pruned trees, parking permits and rubbish, finally realise that the Council isn't listening to them. It listens to wealthy developers, whose 'needs' they prioritise over those of the people who elected them.

Some people worked up alternative schemes, including the 'Hitchcock Kensington', which would have preserved the main theatre, lobby, staircase and much of the Art Deco fabric, adding space to the rear to create a performing arts centre and small hotel in place of the neighbouring former post office site. Despite all this activity, however – which included numerous iterations, a change of ownership and countless planning meetings later – the developer had their permission – as long as they saved part of the facade. After the main buildings were demolished, the precious relic was left exposed to wind, rain and extremes of temperature for six years. It was hardly surprising, then, that this fragment became eroded. Now the Council will have to oversee the like-for-like replacement of the original facade. While this is a statutory obligation, it is yet another disappointing step in the Disneyfication of the Royal Borough, which is a huge threat to so many original, much cherished buildings.

The fate of Kensington Odeon's facade could be taken as a sad metaphor for the degradation of RBKC Council in recent years. A well-built, functional and historic entity, gutted for profit so that overseas buyers could park their dark money there via 'buy to leave' units they have no intention of ever living in, and the precious vestige of the Council left to rot until it crumbled. And now a facsimile must be reinstated to implant a fake memory of Kensington's social, cultural and architectural history.

The venality that has been incorporated into Council aspirations, targets and policies has been given a shiny new facade through the expert, and expensive, ministrations of highly paid imported senior advisers and RBKC's very well-funded Corporate Media and Communications team. After Grenfell, the Council has been on the defensive, spending millions on face-saving PR in addition to huge legal bills for representation – all at the expense of Council taxpayers.

But all is not lost. There are other ways for local authorities to conduct their statutory business, and there are better ways to work with disaffected residents. A brief review of more optimistic and forward-thinking campaigning gives us hope. We have seen how certain unwelcome planning applications and proposals have been knocked back by tough and relentless campaigning. If adversity brings out the best in people, in Kensington, when residents work together, it can change history.

We have seen how Carnival rose from the ashes of race riots and the first racially motivated murder in the UK, that of Kelso Cochrane. His memory is recalled every year at the library near the site of his murder and is part of our incredible history of community rebirth after tragedy, misfortune and human-made catastrophe.

In the early 1970s there were numerous empty properties along

Freston Road that were in disrepair. There were also numerous homeless people, and a group of about 200 people moved into these homes, forming an extensive squat. The squat was run on community principles, and it was a tightly knit group who repaired the houses and set up their own rules and regulations for communal living. In 1974 they declared it the Independent State of Frestonia. It was recognised by the Greater London Council. They had their own identity cards and stamps, and joined the European Union. Over the years some members moved away and the original principles of the group became watered down. Eventually they negotiated with Notting Hill Housing to hand over the land in exchange for new permanent homes on site. Unusually, Notting Hill agreed, then kept its word and the new homes were built. Some of the original Frestonians still live there, and the modest and well-designed homes are testament to good community relations for the benefit of all, won after a long and determined battle. Another hard-won campaign.

In the early 1970s the A40 Westway flyover was built. It cut a swathe through North Kensington's residential streets, enticing drivers from West London and beyond to avoid the Tube and instead speed direct into Baker Street and central London. It caused innumerable problems for areas that it had cut off, including relentless noise and air pollution. The devastation caused by years of demolition and rebuilding meant that the streets to the north of the Westway between Portobello Road and the railway were chopped off to the south and lost their identity. Many properties in the area were in serious disrepair. Residents got together and demanded that the Council step in. They wanted change. After months of failed negotiations, a meeting was agreed between the community, Council officers and Councillors in a hall in North Kensington. Talks did not go well. In the end residents blockaded Council staff and Councillors in the building, where they were forced to stay all night. They were only let out in the morning once terms had been agreed.

The result was the total demolition and rebuilding – as demanded by residents, and agreed and implemented by the Council – of what is now the Swinbrook estate. It had an architecturally positive relationship to the Westway, with a barrier block on Acklam Road that had circulation space bordering the flyover and living space on the opposite side, with large balconies for each flat, often bursting with plants and flowers. The street houses are spacious, light and well laid out internally, and the design won prizes for architects Miller Tritton. It is still considered to be a highly successful neighbourhood design – despite periods of neglect of repairs and maintenance.

More projects, large and small, have been won by communities over the years. When an unwelcome planning application is on the horizon, neighbours and amenity groups come together to object. As we have seen, since 2017 a library and local further education college have been saved by community action. Other victories have been Newcombe House in Notting Hill Gate and Kensington Forum Hotel in Gloucester Road. When unwelcome infrastructure – like the Chelsea Crossrail 2 station on King's Road – is proposed, residents of Council flats and mansion flats come together to object. Amazing things can happen when people work together – so why does the Council fight this invaluable resource?

The faces and the voices of residents of Kensington may be different, but they have a common message: don't destroy our community for profit. Chelsea rose up against the threat to King's Road and the potential level of development that was needed to 'pay for improvements' that residents were not prepared to accept. Angry words were exchanged at Chelsea Old Town Hall between a group of Chelsea's 'pearl-toting matrons' and senior Councillors who wished to support the station.

A week later, angry voices were heard at the Tabernacle in North Kensington. The Westway Trust, set up to compensate residents for the damage done by the Westway, were planning to redevelop and monetise the 23 acres of land they hold for the benefit of local people. Again, a level of development was proposed to 'pay for improvements'.

At two meetings, the people spoke with one voice.

In the first case, after fierce campaigning, the plan for a Chelsea Crossrail station in King's Road was stopped in 2016. After direct action and diplomatic engagement over many years, the development near the Westway was stopped and the leaders of Westway23 campaign group were put in charge of the Westway Trust board in 2021.

We have seen what local activists can achieve – from the squatters of Frestonia to the founders of Carnival and the campaigners for new social housing at Swinbrook. The 'pearl-toting matrons of Chelsea' are as indomitable as the Westway23 organisation, which worked on six campaigns from 2013 to fight the RBKC-driven development juggernaut.

It is a shame that so many K&C residents see themselves as being in permanent opposition to the Council. The Council chamber has been invaded several times over the years by protestors wishing to save nurseries, libraries and Council buildings – and by residents after Grenfell. There may be marches, small interventions, direct action. On occasion, public order laws are broken. Who is working for whom? The balance of power seems to be tipped in favour of 'the executive' and they do their best to keep it that way by managing residents' frustrations and expectations, rather than managing their services better so that they meet the reasonable expectations of those who pay their wages. There have been many times that the Council could have used its discretion and sided with residents, but it chose not to. It sometimes feels like a war.

Kensington and Chelsea Council could do so much better if it realised that if it treated all residents as first-class citizens, residents would be their allies for positive change, rather than enemies of unwelcome development. Even with the vast reserves the Council has had access to over the years – even two years into the pandemic it still has access to considerable amounts of funding – it has regularly failed K&C residents. In some instances, quite spectacularly, as we have seen. At times the Council acts as an agitator to drive a wedge between the unequal communities that it itself has created.

We can only judge the Council's failures by understanding what it prioritises spending money on, how much it has squirrelled away in usable reserves, what its statutory obligations and 'moral' obligations are – especially post-Grenfell – and what mechanisms are available to challenge this. How can we shift the Council away from providing a technocratic response to human problems? But the Council has become a huge impenetrable corporate mass where one team passes the buck to the other and effective scrutiny becomes complex and labyrinthine. I can't help but think this is deliberate.

*

In this book I have attempted to redress this balance by reflecting on some bizarre and unforgivable instances of poor decision-making. The first step is to get accurate information, if that is available. If not, you can pursue it via Freedom of Information requests. The Council's propensity for silo working has been regularly criticised by outside bodies, but this has not improved, even after feedback. This is a failure of leadership that has been pointed out numerous times. Another of the recommendations made to the Council by outside bodies since June 2017 has been to make information more accessible. The Council has failed to do so. The Council website is still impenetrable, and it takes months to update information.

In 2020 the annual budget, which was under public consultation to 186,000 residents for eight weeks, attracted just sixteen comments. The Council cannot claim to have consulted the public if only 16 out of 186,000 residents commented. This is a farce. Kensington and Chelsea deserves so much better.

Despite – or perhaps because of – the poor engagement between the Council and so many of those it is elected to serve, and because residents are used to filling the gaps in the Council's services, the community rose spectacularly to the challenge of the Grenfell Tower atrocity. By all accounts – including the five reports by the government-appointed Independent Grenfell Recovery Taskforce – the community stepped up while the Council stepped down: sometimes in fear, sometimes in disgust, sometimes in ineptitude. A senior Council officer was ordered by the government to visit the site of the disaster, which he had been avoiding. He responded, 'I'm not going, it's like little Africa down there.' You have to wonder about why such a person was appointed to help run the Council. A former MP saw traumatised families and groups of friends made homeless by the Grenfell Tower fire walking the streets one hot night, and judged them to be 'gangs'. Being insulated from the feelings and experiences of the ordinary and extraordinary people they were appointed to serve excludes Councillors from any genuine feelings of compassion, or indeed of racism, which they are often accused of.

It's so interesting to note how the disparate communities in the borough responded to the fire. Some sent teams with freshly cooked food every night. Some sent trauma counsellors. Some came to help sort and deliver clothing and food to people who had been allocated hotels. Several people I know came from their very comfortable homes, rolled up their sleeves and pitched in with whatever was needed. One local celebrity arrived in a limousine and offered to help with 'anything'. They were very happy to spend that day cleaning toilets, which was desperately needed with so many people crowded into the rescue centre. And this person came regularly, happy to do whatever was needed, happy to melt into the background without being recognised.

There are numerous residents with considerable wealth in the borough – as elsewhere in the country, I'm sure – who work hard and use their money for humanitarian projects. During the pandemic I became aware of the work of Millionaires for Humanity, a campaign that started in northern Europe but is now worldwide. It campaigns for a 1% wealth tax – wealth, not income – on everything. And until its campaign is successful each member donates 1% of their wealth annually to a needy cause, currently the worldwide CoVax programme which provides Covid vaccinations to developing countries. We have several members of Millionaires for Humanity in the borough, and I applaud them.

My position on wealthy residents is this: pay your tax at the amount demanded, in the country it was earned; pay your staff properly – look after them and ensure they are employed with good terms and conditions, and treat them with courtesy. Our Exchequer would be far better funded if we had more millionaires who subscribed to this.

Perhaps one downside of paying senior Council executives and directors at a 'competitive' rate of pay (one that is similar to a salary they could achieve in the commercial world) is that they think they are corporate executives and that lowly Councillors and residents are their employees. On numerous occasions residents have accused the Council of behaving like a corporation rather than an accountable public body. On several instances I and other outspoken Councillors have been berated – once formally by the CEO, and threatened with disciplinary procedures – for 'disloyalty', when in fact scrutinising and passing informed criticism on the decision-making priorities at RBKC is part of our job. It is quite simply anti-democratic for senior officers to demand that opposition Councillors toe the Council's line; it is a total misunderstanding of our role. I reminded the senior officer concerned that I didn't work for him. I don't think he liked it.

Some of us have joked about those in authority at RBKC taking training for 'empathy and advanced platitudes', but I have heard that some people have indeed taken training, as they have absolutely no idea how to deal with basic human reactions, let alone deal with people who are traumatised and bereaved. Sometimes people who are afraid, or frustrated, or aren't being listened to, speak loudly. It is not necessarily an act of aggression. Yet 'loud voices' are regularly criticised by those in authority. In fact, ignoring the pleas of people who are desperate for you to listen to them, treating them with condescension and platitudes instead of responding genuinely, is a form of aggression that has no place in an elected authority that is supposed to be accountable to those it represents.

There is another way. Our activist history in Kensington and Chelsea is extraordinary. And alternative ways of working have proved successful elsewhere.

A Town and Country Planning Association review of changes in planning policy, 'Planning Out Poverty', was published in 2011 and has been updated numerous times. It revealed how recent amendments in national planning policy had removed the imperative to include responsibilities relating to improving equity, and replaced them with a focus on design and 'inclusive places' for social interaction.

To my mind, good planning should focus on what people consider to be precious, what is valued, what is special and idiosyncratic, what is utterly and unquestionably not to be messed with. Then good planning should preserve it. Save it. Improve it. Grow it. Make it better and more profitable to the people who run it.

Preserve, nurture and intensify what is good.

When you've done that, you may then nibble around the edges and slide in some extra housing. But don't be greedy. Do enough, but don't do too much. People will know. If you're not greedy, if you don't go too far, you won't kill the thing you hope to profit from and annihilate the community you rely on.

However, the Council has too often interpreted 'planning policy' as referring to coffee shops and security-controlled parks rather than realising that there should be widely accessible and free-to-use social spaces, community rooms, libraries, schools and primary care in a neighbourhood. This has meant that publicly owned areas that had been free to use were replaced by monetised spaces, and this increased the process of squeezing out – or social cleansing – people who cannot afford £7 for a cup of coffee. National planning objectives have shifted away from creating equality, social justice and a healthy environment for all communities. Instead the job of planning officers has become to enable development using the euphemistically titled 'development control' which, after the 'presumption to approve', which meant that some applications would be approved automatically, government policy was implemented, undermining the sovereignty of Planning Committees. A generation of these developer- and profit-friendly priorities has given us cold, damp, mouldy, poorly constructed and low-quality new homes with questionable fire safety standards. And of course, in the end it gave us Grenfell.

It has created a planning process that does not cater for low-income families, who are the nuts and bolts of society. This process has slowly driven them out of the borough into 'permanent temporary' accommodation, or – worse – poor-quality overpriced private rented homes.

Instead of this short-termism and the emphasis on delivering luxury empty homes – 'homes for nobody' – at vast profit, we need long-term thinking that focuses on improving outcomes for education, health, housing and work and that considers our small children, young people, working families and elders, creating a level playing field by accommodating their changing aspirations and needs. There are some excellent examples. They can be achieved by a people-focused planning system, but also by taking a fresh approach to local health provision. Yet the Council ignored my evidence-backed report on inequality, and even a report by the highly respected Kensington and Chelsea Foundation on similar issues. I expected a response. But no. The Council is not interested in tackling inequality. End of. But we must change this.

In 2016 I read about a transformative, holistic approach to healthcare that began with an initiative in Frome in Somerset. This became known as the Compassionate Frome framework. A local GP, seeing the extent to which social isolation was affecting the physical health and general well-being of her patients, decided to do something about it. She started by recommending that elderly or isolated patients should attend groups, classes and events. It was highly successful; this was the beginning of social prescribing. Over the next few years, the project expanded to cover the county. The project was taken up formally by the local health authority, which mapped community resources and found ways to develop them where there were gaps, or where services or voluntary organisations needed support. They worked with these organisations as partners. They focused on the specific needs of each patient and matched their needs with appropriate help, where possible, especially around patient discharge from hospitals, which is always a difficult transition if support isn't there.

They set up a 'care coordination hub' and worked alongside GP and medical services, ensuring genuine wraparound and entirely people-centred care, with a training programme for clinicians to help them understand and work with the new philosophy. They worked with young people to ensure they had similar support, including opportunities for volunteering. It was systematic, proactive and holistic.

They also had support for unpaid carers, including child carers, giving them enough information and support to help them make decisions themselves, especially those who were caring for family members with long-term conditions. They provided backup to clinicians – who don't always have the time or capacity to offer support for non-medical conditions – 'restoring genuine care and compassionate, patient-centred care'. They worked with a 'compassionate community' ethos. They organised 'healthy Mondays' at 'talking cafes' where people could go, eat a healthy meal and speak to others who felt isolated.

Not only did people feel better and more positive, but their physical health actually improved – measurably. In time there was a reduction in admissions to A&E, a decrease in the use of medication for certain chronic illnesses, and a reduction in the number of GP appointments booked. Numerous organisations across the country have since taken on the Compassionate Frome framework and Compassionate Communities now exist in all corners of the country. Various organisations cater for the needs of their communities, particularly in the areas of social care and palliative care.

Frome Town Council run 'Fair Frome'. This scheme 'champions greater financial, educational, social and health equality for people living in Frome and the surrounding areas . . . working to create joined-up, sustainable services across Frome'. Fair Frome uses local businesses and local employees, and contracts, services and materials are purchased locally by the Council so that money is recirculated locally. It's a well-known framework: local procurement is known to benefit local businesses, building wealth in the local community.

Preston Council has also become well known for committing

to procure and commission locally: the Council Leader has written and spoken about its success for some years. The Council is the 'place leader', promoting its approach to other 'anchor institutions' as well as the private sector. This includes local colleges, universities, housing associations, local police and Lancashire County Council. The model helps local people ensure that the benefits of growth are invested locally. Manchester pioneered progressive procurement some years ago, and many other places are involved in similar schemes to keep investment in the local area and avoid profit being skimmed off into the pockets of large corporations based elsewhere.

In late 2021 it was judged that according to the National Institute for Health Research, Preston had coped far better with the pandemic than areas that had not taken community wealth-building and the Compassionate Communities concept on board.

We can hardly pretend that Kensington and Chelsea Council is following Frome or Preston, though they are happy to embrace small acts of community wealth-building – usually tokenistic then over-promoted. Many communities are already very well connected, whether via interest groups, religious practices, ethnic groups or indeed by a shared opposition to something going on in their neighbourhood. The Council has been advised, over and again, by outside bodies, to capitalise on, and learn from, existing networks. Its mistake is often that it seems to want to take over these networks, to change, dilute and control them, rather than support them to grow independently.

Kensington has always had a strong religious network (of churches, mosques, the gurdwara and Holland Park Synagogue) and network of social groups, ethnic groups, groups with common interests. The compassion network is widespread and works hard, though it is little recognised and often all but invisible. I still find it extraordinary that our voluntary organisations, who have all but taken over many front-line services in the borough, have to beg every year for funding, for which they are then expected to be subserviently grateful. They should be treated – and some have asked to be treated – as equal partners rather than having to enter a transactional relationship where they are kept 'in their place' as supplicants rather than equal partners, cooperative providers of services the Council should be providing, for which they are rewarded with a photo op with the mayor and a pat on the head.

The idea that some people genuinely consider that 'Food banks are a fine and noble thing' is reprehensible in an area of both extreme wealth and food poverty. Some people just want to salve their conscience while maintaining the social hierarchy. In a good society that is well run, there should be no need for charities – but here we are.

The amazing network of mutual help, support and love post-Grenfell has come about because of the Council's failure to provide it. This is not new: this failure existed before the fire and it existed before local campaign groups got together to fight unwelcome development. This happens in areas like ours because we are naturally neighbourly; long-term residents live cheek by jowl. In my block of ten terraced houses (five each side and split into flats) many of us have lived there as long as I have – thirty-five years. Many have been there for ten, fifteen or twenty years. There are very few homes with a high turnover of occupants. We look after each other. When I was ill, and during the lockdowns, I almost had to fight off neighbours offering to do my shopping. Flat battery? Neighbours will run out of their homes to help. We have millionaires and retired social tenants on our road, but most of all we are neighbours. And that feeling of responsibility for each other is multiplied across North Kensington.

It might be interesting to consider how betrayed people feel by an organisation that is actually paid to care for us, but has failed spectacularly to do so. The Council isn't just there to empty bins, sweep the streets and plant exotic non-native trees in every nook and corner. We expect our elected representatives, and those who work for them, to abide by a mutually accepted social contract. As Jean-Jacques Rousseau put it:

> Individuals have consented, explicitly or tacitly, to surrender some of their freedoms and submit to the authority (of the ruler, or to the decision of a majority) in exchange for protection of their remaining rights or maintenance of the social order.

If we believe, as many do, that the social contract that should exist between the people and the Council has been broken, a case can surely be made to challenge the status quo and to find a way to change it. We clearly have the means to do so, with proactive residents' groups that could form an effective People's Council or some other means by which residents could work with the Council to ensure that services are offered not as reluctant concessions but as the Council's public duty, offered unconditionally and with robust and proactive compassion.

Is the Council capable of such change?

In K&C Council, as we have seen, the status quo over the years allowed tens of millions of pounds to be spent on vanity projects

– some of little value, either socially or financially – while residents in deprived areas in West Chelsea and in North Kensington have struggled to put food on the table or buy school uniform for their families. Malnutrition in these areas has worsened and the Council's response, which was to make patronising comments about better nutrition, means nothing if it doesn't then take steps to tackle poverty wages and welfare payments.

Instead the Council focused on development for gain, and allowed social tenants to die. It is shameful to think that, five years after the fire, in full knowledge of the inequality that exists and what can happen when it is ignored, in every single ward in K&C we have elders living in poverty. Every one. I wonder how the borough's malnourished children will end their days, suffering all the conditions that poverty and deprivation can cause, in addition to possible trauma from the Grenfell Tower fire and chronic illness or other effects from the pandemic. I've sat in my Councillor surgery many times and seen people coming in on crutches or in a wheelchair, younger than me but with a list of health problems that will shorten their life and reduce the quality of their life.

The Council calls it 'building resilience' but cutting funding to local voluntary organisations – the people who are providing local core services the Council has withdrawn – is a deliberate process of managed decline, not of improving efficiency.

The Council's patriarchal attitude to funding the voluntary organisations that are holding our communities together means it can disguise the failures and weaknesses of the local authority. The Council is determined to maintain the hierarchy that permits them to treat the funding accumulated by council tax, local taxes and charges, and government funding as if it is its own money. I often say to residents, 'It is YOUR money they are misspending or withholding and demanding your thanks for. YOUR MONEY.'

Having talked to friends from many different councils around London and around the country, it is clear to me that the archaic way in which the RBKC Council functions is neither traditional nor charming. It has been, and can be, dangerous. The Triborough project was instigated with no consultation – not even a bad consultation process, but none at all. Labour Councillors literally heard about it on BBC news, and were told that there was to be no input from opposition Councillors. With no checks and balances in place, no scrutiny whatsoever until something went awry, the blame for the failures of this '£100 million efficiency drive' lies squarely with the then leadership of H&F, K&C and Westminster councils. It cost us tens of millions of pounds, and we are not even allowed to question these sums as some of the contracts are still undergoing legal inquiries, which is also costing taxpayers dearly. The complexities of these multi-borough contracts can be judged by the years of legal unpicking that continues; we may never know how much the Councils lost in funding, services and reputation through this ill-judged and poorly planned 'efficiency drive'.

It is not just campaigners from North Ken who are treated like the enemy. Amenity groups and RAs in wealthier parts of the borough are also treated with disdain – albeit more politely. The Council seems power-mad and obsessed with secrecy. It also seems determined to learn no lessons from its mistakes, and even to repeat its worst mistakes. It could even be failing in its statutory duties.

Compassion does not mean simply an absence of personal abuse or vindictiveness. It cannot be passive. Compassion in action – as is well known by so many voluntary organisations, religious and community groups – is active. It cares for people without judgement. It is not transactional. But unless that compassion incorporates actions to change the status quo, whether this is via party political change or the drive of local communities, we are complicit in maintaining the failing status quo and ensuring the long-term survival of the broken system.

We cannot be passive bystanders in a world that creates such unspeakable inequity. We should not simply pity those who have been failed; we should take action to initiate a programme of change. To be an agent of change. We need strategy, implementation and continuous improvement.

Inequality to the extent we see in K&C is not a natural consequence. To counter this we must first alleviate people's immediate suffering; understand and acknowledge the failures that have created or allowed this to happen; identify changes that can be made locally; and finally, lobby and fight for change at a London-wide or a national level.

Forcing more people into being dependent on benefits, squeezing wages and job security, affects physical and mental health. It makes people feel disenfranchised and disempowered. It is also bad for the economy – local, London-wide and national.

Systemic failure can only be redressed with systemic change: to achieve that, we need active citizens who have agency in their own destiny.

People from all over the borough have a lot of common ground. We care about each other, we want the best for each other, and we enjoy the diversity of our communities and how we function and live side by side. We can set aside our differences and make things run better – for all of us. Our wonderful communities are well able to do this, and I would love to see them come forward as active citizens to improve life for everyone.

Kensington deserves better.

And this is my love letter to Kensington.

EPILOGUE

The sight of RBKC Council positioning itself in advance of its appearance at the Grenfell Inquiry in May 2021 was disheartening.

At the time, Councillors were sent daily news updates, carefully curated to present a corporate face a little less disingenuous than the reality. The Council insisted on calling the Grenfell Tower fire a 'tragedy', as if it was some kind of natural disaster. As one Tory Councillor said: 'These things happen.' Well, no, they don't. The community says the fire was an 'atrocity': it had been predicted, it was entirely avoidable, and the Council's emergency response was lamentable. However, in this Council briefing session in May 2021 we were encouraged to note the 'tone' of the Council's QC during his opening statement, in comparison to that of KCTMO. This ignored what we all know: that the Council's legal team, costing £4.5 million a year, which the Council hired with tax-payers' money, is way beyond the financial capacity of what is left of KCTMO. Hiring a better QC will buy you a better performer, but it does not make you any more, or less, responsible.

The current Council political leadership team appear to have been trained to repeat endless meaningless apologies, performative empathy and splendid platitudes, though sometimes their impatience leaks out. In reality, they are little better than the contemptible former leadership, who presided over the worst peacetime disaster of our lives. Some, I was informed, were appointed by the government, though this seems unlikely given their lack of talent and skills, for which they attempt to compensate by using one of their highly paid new directors as a human shield when things go wrong.

From the earliest days after the fire, many residents demanded that the Council should be put into special measures. Some still do.

The Council still puts financial profit before community benefit. To compensate for their Councillors' lack of skills and relevant experience, they appoint more and more directors – nearly three times more than Hammersmith & Fulham Council, which has a larger population and more modest reserves, but is far better run without a bloated directorship.

I understand that many residents are unaware of these issues. For those people, whose only contact with the Council relates to bin collection, or parking, or tree trimming, and they see all these things running pretty well, it comes as a shock when they enter the battleground and meet the hard, bureaucratic face of the Council. This might be on a planning issue, where they become hugely frustrated by the Council's intransigence. Such residents are genuinely surprised to discover that the Council does not work for them, but for faceless developers on behalf of a deeply embedded trickle-up economy. The language used by resident protestors at the Planning Committee meeting for South Kensington Station in December 2021 was typical. The local Residents' Association representatives berated the Council for favouring overdevelopment rather than maintaining the character of the neighbourhood, telling them: 'You are pandering to developers.' They sounded just like us in North Ken.

The Council is responsible for multiple failures, missteps and poor judgement, while outside Kensington Town Hall we have communities with such humanity, such care, so many and varied skills, such useful links to expertise, and the ability to mobilise. It is this social capital that the Council so often ignores, despite numerous outside bodies begging the Council to watch and listen, to learn from them and to work alongside them. This advice came from the earliest days after the fire, from the Independent Grenfell Taskforce in 2017, and more recently from the Centre for Scrutiny and Governance reports in 2021. Instead the Council employs yet more directors to write policies it will never implement: as one report put it, 'Writing policy as a proxy for action'.

The Council is also inclined to equate any community dissent with an imagined battle between rich and poor, whereas in fact it is more often a clash of values between the people and the Council. They frame it as such to build and maintain distrust between communities, and perhaps even to impose and maintain social control. But they are not mediators in this conflict; they are agitators. The more that our disparate communities mingle, the more we see that this is about principles and values.

Just like many local authorities who have forgotten who they work for, RBKC Council needs a total reset. But the case of RBKC should be a lesson for anyone working in, elected to, or subject to local government – and that means everyone. The Council didn't listen. Seventy-two people died, in the worst way imaginable. And they still don't get it.

Expecting charities to fill the gaps in provision forces them to be complicit in the ongoing failure of the Council to provide services. I remain shocked that the Council is aware of inequalities but does nothing to address them. Let us remember some of their responses to challenges on this. Some years ago when discussing catch-up schemes for children who were falling behind with schoolwork, one Councillor said: 'You can spoil a child with too much education and wealth.' In relation to housing inequality, a former Leader of the Council said: 'Inequality is caused by people who rent scarce private sector accommodation on Housing Benefit in the borough.' Asked why grants to certain voluntary organisations were not forthcoming that year, a senior Councillor said: 'We can't pander to every special interest group . . . it is a slippery slope.' When questioned as to what local benefit there would be from '£1000-handbag shops' in a deprived area, a senior Councillor said residents should 'earn more money and buy handbags'. During a debate on welcoming child refugees from Syria, a Councillor stated, with gritted teeth: 'If we let these children in, we will have an Islamic caliphate in Kensington and Chelsea.'

Let us remember above all that a Council with £0.3 billion in usable reserves chose to cut £276,000 from the cladding costs of a refurbishment project in a 'value engineering' exercise, agreed to use cheaper materials (the new school next to Grenfell Tower used more expensive but not flammable materials), in an economy drive, while spending millions on extending museums and paving Exhibition Road with pink granite from China.

There was no pressing need to economise on the refurbishment of Grenfell Tower. It was an ideological choice.

There is no excuse for the extremes of inequality that exist in our beautiful borough. We can afford to tackle it. It is an ideological choice.

Apologies and tweaks are not enough. We have witnessed catastrophic and systemic failure, and a failure of leadership to acknowledge the immensity of this. The Council has broken the social contract it had with residents, and it is time for citizens to challenge the status quo and make it clear who works for whom.

Why did I write this book? To set the record straight; to demonstrate that the disaster of life-limiting inequalities and the atrocity of the Grenfell Tower fire were avoidable; to get behind the layers of obfuscation and fudge and to clarify what has been, for me, sixteen years of frustration and not being heard. Our communities could do a far better job of guiding and steering the Council than the 'activity but no change' that we have become accustomed to.

On the night of 9 June 2017, outside the Town Hall, when the announcement that I had won the election and had become MP was made to an astonished world, I said: 'Kensington has spoken. Never be silent again.'

Let us all be heard.

ACKNOWLEDGEMENTS

I would like to thank the team at Andrew Nurnberg Associates, in particular Charlotte Merritt, for their enthusiasm on picking up the book, and the various editors at Quercus, in particular Ben Brock, who have seen me through the painstaking editing of the script (some of which still makes me rage or cry), through pandemic and political upheaval.

I would also like to acknowledge the unfailing support of close colleagues Sina Lari and David Kear in Kensington Labour Party and most especially now-retired Councillor Pat Mason, who has been my guide and inspiration over sixteen years.

ACKNOWLEDGMENTS

REFERENCES

Page xii
Grenfell Tower Inquiry Reports:
Phase 1 Report, October 2019: www.grenfelltowerinquiry.org.uk

Page 11
Independent Grenfell Recovery Taskforce:
Initial Report: https://www.gov.uk/government/publications/
initial-report-from-the-independent-recovery-taskforce-31-oc-
tober-2017

Page 24
RBKC Cabinet, Cabinet and Corporate Services Scrutiny
Committee papers, July 2013

Page 25
Chelsea Care Report:
RBKC Cabinet and Corporate Services Scrutiny Committee papers,
October 2011.

Page 33

Nymphs in a Landscape, Andrea Meldolla (partially clothed)
Crenaia, the Nymph of the Dargle, Frederic Lord Leighton (naked)

Page 34

Bentley Continental cost: Channel 4 *Dispatches*, 2013 (bought in 2007)

Page 40

Dates of scrutiny relating to 3B and contracting: Chair of Cabinet and Corporate Services Scrutiny Committee, May 2012 to May 2014

RBKC Procurement Scrutiny Working Group: working under Cabinet and Corporate Services Scrutiny Committee – report published October 2016

Page 61

Hedge funds owning home care business: 'Multinational care companies are the winners', *The Guardian,* 15 September 2021
Healthwatch England report: *The Guardian*, 24 August 2017
'The Most Unequal Borough in Britain', 2014, published by EDC

Page 62

Walk of Shame: Cole Moreton, 'The Walk of Shame', colemoreton. com, 23 February 2015
'Food banks are a fine and noble thing', *Kensington News*, May 2017

Page 63

'After Grenfell: Housing and Inequality in Kensington and Chelsea:

"The most unequal borough in Britain"', November 2017, published by EDC

Page 64
'The most unequal borough in Britain – revisited: Inequality and inequity in Kensington and Chelsea', October 2020, published by EDC

Page 65
'Health Equity in England: The Marmot Review ten years on', February 2020, www.instituteofhealthequity.org
https://www.instituteofhealthequity.org/about-our-work/latest-updates-from-the-institute/build-back-fairer

Page 66
'Poverty and Prosperity in Kensington and Chelsea: Understanding inequality in a borough of extremes', November 2021, WPI Economics for Kensington and Chelsea Foundation, www.thekandcfoundation.com

Page 68
2014 inequality report

Page 74
RBKC Cabinet Report papers, May 2012

Page 77
'Room for Improvement: The handling of casework by registered social landlords', January 2009, published by EDC

Page 78
RBKC Strategic Housing Market Assessment 2009

Page 80
RBKC Housing and Property Committee, September 2010, paper
  A10

Page 81
'Housing in Kensington: Where will your children live?', with
  foreword by Dr Rod Abouharb, April 2015, published by EDC

Page 85
2014 inequality report

Page 87
'After Grenfell – Housing and Inequality in Kensington and Chelsea:
  "The most unequal borough in Britain"', November 2017, pub-
  lished by EDC

Page 90
'Drop the MP: A catalogue of management failure in Kensington
  constituency', January 2019, published by EDC

Page 101
'Understanding the Creative and Cultural Sectors in Kensington
  and Chelsea', BOP Consulting for RBKC, December 2008

Page 103

'Ends and Means: The future roles of social housing in England', John Hills' report for CASE no. 34, February 2007

Page 106

'Principles for Social Housing Reform', Stephen Greenhalgh and John Moss for Localis, 2009

Page 108

Nicholas Boys Smith and Alex Morton, 'Create Streets: not just multi-storey estates', report for Policy Exchange, 2013

Page 110

John Harris, 'Welcome to Toytown: What life is like in new-build Britain', *The* Guardian, 6 April 2013

Page 114

RBKC Housing and Property Committee, Paper A6, 'Proposed Changes to Housing Benefit, Local Housing Allowance and Temporary Accommodation Subsidy', September 2010

Page 118

'Investing in our Housing Stock', report for RBKC by Savill's, April 2013

Page 134

'Investigation Report on Long-Standing Complaints of the Kensington and Chelsea Tenants' Management Organisation', for RBKC by Maria Memoli MBA, April 2009, www.localgovernance.co.uk

Page 139
RBKC Independent Grenfell Taskforce report 1

Page 141
RBKC Independent Grenfell Taskforce report 2

Page 143
RBKC Independent Grenfell Taskforce reports 3 and 4

Page 146
RBKC Independent Grenfell Taskforce report 5

Page 148
Bishop James Jones, 'Charter for Families Bereaved through Public Tragedy' ('Hillsborough Charter'), November 2017

Page 151
'Independent Review of the Kensington Centre Campus Transaction' ('Kroll 1'), October 2018

Page 153
'Independent Review of Property Transactions' ('Kroll 2'), February 2021

Page 158
RBKC Kroll to Audit and Transparency Committee papers, March 2021

Page 159
RBKC Audit and Transparency Committee papers, Grenfell Funding Report A&T, no 1

Page 165
Victoria Borwick MP, survey on Carnival, January 2016

Page 193
Marmot Report update, February 2020
RBKC, Green Paper on Housing, October 2017

Page 195
RBKC Taskforce reports and 'Creating Stronger Communities 2018/19'

Page 197
RBKC Procurement Scrutiny Working Group report 2016

Page 199
RBKC Council Plan 2019/23

Page 215
'Planning Out Poverty: The reinvention of social town planning', Town and Country Planning Association, 2011

Page 217
Inequality 2 plus K&C Foundation report

Page 218

'The health and health inequalities impact of a place-based
Community Wealth Initiative which has become known nation-
ally as "the Preston Model"', National Institute for Health
Research, 24 August 2021